W9-DGG-299

Barbara McClintock

Genius of Genetics

Naomi Pasachoff

Enslow Publishers, Inc.
40 Industrial Road
Box 398
Berkeley Heights, NJ 07922
USA

PO Box 38
Aldershot
Hants GU12 6BP
UK

http://www.enslow.com

Dedication

For my mother, Anna Jacobson Schwartz, as recognized in her field of economics as McClintock was in genetics; at age 90, like McClintock, she still goes every day to her office, where she is working on a new book.

Library of Congress Cataloging-in-Publication Data

Pasachoff, Naomi E.
Barbara McClintock : genius of genetics / by Naomi Pasachoff.
p. cm. — (Great minds of science)
Includes bibliographical references and index.
ISBN 0-7660-2505-5
1. McClintock, Barbara, 1902—Juvenile literature. 2. Women geneticists—United States—Biography—Juvenile literature. I. Title. II. Series.
QH437.5.M38P37 2006
576.5'092—dc22

2005014915

Printed in the United States of America

10 9 8 7 6 5 4 3 2 1

To Our Readers:
We have done our best to make sure all Internet Addresses in this book were active and appropriate when we went to press. However, the author and the publisher have no control over and assume no liability for the material available on those Internet sites or on other Web sites they may link to. Any comments or suggestions can be sent by e-mail to comments@enslow.com or to the address on the back cover.

Illustration Credits: All images courtesy of the Cold Spring Harbor Laboratory, except pp. 28 and 73, courtesy the National Library of Medicine, and p. 35, Division of Rare and Manuscript Collections, Carl A. Kroch Library, Cornell University.

Cover Illustration: JupiterImages Corporation (background); Cold Spring Harbor Laboratory (foreground portrait).

Contents

Acknowledgments

Barbara McClintock: Genius of Genetics is my fourth book for Enslow Publishers. I have been lucky enough to have the same editor throughout my association with the firm. I want to thank him for all his assistance in general and for giving me the opportunity to stretch myself in this case in particular. With a background stronger in the physical sciences than in the life sciences, I have been happy to extend my vocabulary with this project to include terms like transposons, epigenetics, and haploids.

Ever since I became an author, I have been lucky enough to find colleagues who were prepared to share their expertise with me. None of my previous books, however, benefited so much from the assistance of a single individual as this biography of Barbara McClintock.

In autumn 2004 I contacted Cornell University archivist Elaine Engst to ask for advice on how to proceed with my new project on McClintock, who had been educated at Cornell. Engst was kind enough to put me in touch with Lee B. Kass, a scholar who is preparing an intellectual biography of McClintock. Without Kass's help, I would not have been aware of the exciting new developments in McClintock scholarship, most of which are the result of her indefatigable research. She is the first to use documentary evidence from around the country to establish the true facts of McClintock's education and career. In the process of doing so, she has successfully debunked many of the myths that have been told about McClintock for over a quarter-century.

Some of Kass's research appears first in the Maize Genetics Cooperation Newsletter. As Kass has pointed out, from its beginnings over 70 years ago, the participants in the Maize Genetics Cooperation have graciously shared their research with one another. Kass herself is clearly imbued with a similar spirit. My gratitude to her knows no bounds.

Among the books that Kass suggested I read was an excellent 2003 biography by Maxine Singer and Paul Berg of McClintock's colleague and friend George Beadle. Singer, president emeritus of the Carnegie Institution of Washington (1988-2002), answered some questions I posed to her by e-mail about the workings of the institution.

In addition to alerting me to recently published books on related subjects and to her many articles, Kass introduced me via e-mail to one of McClintock's younger colleagues and closest associates, Nina V. Fedoroff. Fedoroff, too, proved extremely generous with her time and knowledge and helped answer my many questions about McClintock's science. Like Kass, she read the book in manuscript form and made both necessary corrections and helpful suggestions.

At Fedoroff's urging, I also showed the manuscript to two other McClintock associates. Both David Botstein, director of the Lewis-Sigler Institute for Integrative Genomics at Princeton University (and coincidentally my husband's high-school and college classmate), and Evelyn Witkin, Barbara McClintock Professor of Genetics Emeritus at Rutgers University, took the time to read the draft and to say nice things about it.

I was also lucky to have help from individuals at Cold Spring Harbor Lab. My friend and unofficial life sciences consultant Alfred Goldberg, a professor of cell biology at the Harvard Medical School, put me in touch with Mila Pollock, the Cold Spring Harbor archivist. She, in turn, gave me the name of the lab's director of media relations, Peter Sherwood. I am grateful to them for their assistance.

Invaluable support was also available at Williams College, my home institution. Geneticist Marsha Altschuler, chair of the biology department and a Cornell Ph.D. herself, was willing to respond to my many queries and suggest miscellaneous readings. Agnes Demianski, a plant geneticist at Monsanto in St. Louis and the daughter of a visiting professor of astronomy at Williams, was the first of my many readers. Thanks to her careful reading and encouraging comments, I started to believe that I could do justice after all to the complicated story of McClintock's life and work. Williams reference librarians, especially Jodi A. Psoter and Rebecca Ohm, assisted me in tracking down a variety of research materials. My friend Susan Dunn, professor of humanities at Williams, kept my spirits up while I struggled with complicated issues in genetics.

Other friends and family members also assisted in a variety of ways. My friend Peter Lipton, Head of the Department of History and Philosophy of Science at Cambridge University, offered both helpful suggestions and words of encouragement after reading an early version of the manuscript. Dorothy Segal, whom I have known since 1969, when we were both editorial assistants in the School English Department at Houghton Mifflin Company, also did a careful reading of an early draft. My husband, daughters, son-in-law, sister, and mother all helped sustain me in various ways while I worked on the project. I hope I can repay their kindnesses someday.

The Original Big Mac

A GOOD SEVEN YEARS BEFORE THE FIRST fast-food restaurant with golden arches opened in the United States, there was already a Big Mac. The original Big Mac, however, was not an all-beef patty sandwich on a sesame-seed bun. Rather, she was a petite, short-haired, bespectacled woman, in her late forties. By 1948 Big Mac had already made a name for herself as a major figure in the field of genetics, the science of heredity. In particular, she was a cytogeneticist. "Cyto" means "cell"—the basic unit of all organisms. Cytogeneticists uncover facts about genetics by studying the cells of living organisms with microscopes. Big Mac was one of the first to apply the techniques of cytogenetics to the study of maize, or Indian corn. She had been engaged in this labor of love for over two decades, dating back to her student years at Cornell University. In recognition of her achievements, she had become, in 1944, the third woman ever elected to the National Academy of Sciences, and, in 1945, the first woman ever elected president of the Genetics Society of America.

Why had a group of Barbara McClintock's fellow scientists given her that particular nickname? As one of her younger colleagues explained almost forty-five years later, the answer lay in the jeans outfit she wore while working in her corn field. "There was nothing unusual about this outfit except for the buttons on the denim jacket she usually wore. The buttons were made of brass and embossed on their outer surface in large letters was the brand name, *Big Mac!* To those of us who as students and associates knew Barbara's research and the enormous impact her cytogenetic studies in maize had made on the field of genetics in the 1930s and 1940s, those buttons were most appropriate. For us she was *the* original *Big Mac!*"[1]

Even the most dedicated fast-food fans might do a double take if they learned that their favorite meal had won an award. In October 1983, however, Barbara McClintock's fans knew that she deserved to become the first woman ever to win an unshared Nobel Prize in physiology or medicine (the official name of the prize, including the "or"). This Nobel Prize is the highest award any life scientist can aspire to. In the ten or so years leading up to her Nobel Prize, McClintock had also been awarded a number of other distinguished prizes.

In between 1948, however, when McClintock acquired the nickname Big Mac, and the 1980s, when she began to collect prestigious awards, McClintock's work was not as enthusiastically embraced as she had hoped. Her discovery of "mobile genetic elements," the work for which she was honored with the Nobel Prize, was not immediately hailed beyond the plant genetics community. Since her reputation was that of a meticulously careful researcher, other scientists did not dismiss her discovery. For a variety of reasons, however, they did not know what to do with it.

Why did McClintock's "jumping genes," as they were known popularly, fail to be taken very seriously by the scientific community as a whole? One reason was that they did not fit in with the picture of the genome that geneticists had been patiently sketching over the decades of the twentieth century. The genome is the library of genetic information that determines the development of living organisms. Geneticists had come to believe that the genome was made up of threadlike bodies called chromosomes, and that chromosomes carry genes that hold stable positions in a line. As one of McClintock's younger colleagues and closest associates later put it, "when Barbara McClintock announced in 1948 that genes could move from one place to another, it was tantamount to saying the kitchen could occasionally move into the attic. Geneticists—McClintock among them—had been mapping [the positions of] genes [on chromosomes] for decades. They knew very well that genes maintained their locations—maps couldn't be made if genes moved around all the time. Genes had fixed locations, like beads on a string, and their order along the chromosomes could be counted on generation after generation."[2]

Only over a period of decades did the wide-ranging significance of the work that earned her the Nobel Prize become apparent. In the 1960s and 1970s, decades after McClintock first discovered them in maize, "jumping genes" were discovered in a variety of organisms by younger scientists using the new instruments and techniques of molecular biology. Molecular biologists study the molecules that direct molecular processes in cells. For example, large molecules in the cells of organisms store genetic information. Molecular biologists study how these molecules convert that information into chemical reactions that can determine an organism's traits.

Opening Up New Fields of Research

Once it became apparent that mobile genetic elements were a common feature of organisms, and not something peculiar only to McClintock's corn, their importance to public health soon became apparent. Scientists were now able to explain why bacteria seemed to develop resistance to antibiotics almost as quickly as new ones hit the market. The concept of "transposition"—that genes could move over generations from one place on the genome to another and even from one type of organism to another—also shed new light on the field of evolution. Perhaps transposable genetic elements helped contribute to the development of new species over time.

New applications of her work continue to astonish scientists even today, more than a half century later.

Nobel Prize-winning geneticist Barbara McClintock.

McClintock used the term "controlling elements" for what others dubbed "jumping genes." She believed that the movement of genetic material might control development in general. Scientists knew that all the cells of an organism contain the same genetic information. Why, then, did certain cells go on to become liver cells, for example, and others skin cells? Perhaps the answer lay in controlling elements, which seemed to act like switches. Depending on whether certain switches were activated or deactivated, cells developed one way or another. If this were true, genetic switches might control the development of life.

The specifics of McClintock's theory of controlling elements have not proven accurate. Her concept of genetic switches, however, has opened up entire fields of twenty-first-century research. One new research area, epigenetics, studies the way some human diseases result from inappropriate gene silencing while other diseases are caused by inappropriate gene activation. Another new research field, focusing on so-called small RNAs, studies the way this class of molecule can upset genetic programming by shutting down genes completely or regulating them in some other way. Findings from both of these areas of research help to explain how two cells containing the same genetic material can have two different fates.

Even McClintock's earlier work underlies important medical research today. Her discovery of controlling elements resulted from years of carefully studying what happens to chromosomes when they are broken by different types of stress. She was particularly interested in telomeres, the protective caps at the ends of chromosomes. Scientists have since learned that telomeres are maintained by a protein—telomerase—that causes chemical changes. Both aging and cancer seem to be affected by loss of telomere stability due to improper telomerase activity. Thus McClintock's work with telomeres may prove crucial both to an understanding of the aging process and to the discovery of new therapies to treat cancer.

Reacting to Rejection

One measure of the greatness of a scientist's work is how many new areas of research it opens up. On these grounds, McClintock's work is clearly of the highest order. A measure of a scientist as a human being, however, is a more difficult thing to gauge. McClintock's behavior during the decades when she felt shunned by her peers says much about her character. When very few scientists seemed interested in reading about her research, she continued to work carefully in her corn fields and in her laboratory. She continued to write up her research as if she were submitting it for publication. Then, instead of actually sending her articles off to journals, she filled the file cabinets in her office with her detailed reports. Her only official publications over many years were the annual summary reports she dutifully submitted to the yearbook of the Carnegie Institution of Washington, the unique scientific organization that supported McClintock's work for over half a century. Despite her dismay at her seeming inability to communicate the value of her efforts, she continued to take pleasure in her daily work.

Barbara McClintock is hardly the only scientist in history to experience rejection. Unlike some, in fact, she was lucky enough to live to see her work and ideas celebrated. By contrast, Gregor Mendel, the so-called Father of Genetics, died in 1884 without the satisfaction of knowing that his research would lay the groundwork for an entire field of study. When awards began to be showered upon Barbara McClintock, who never cared for publicity or money, she took little satisfaction in the public acclaim or in the material rewards that they brought along with them. Getting dressed up for a formal dinner was not McClintock's thing. She much preferred her typical everyday uniform—tan chinos with a short-sleeved white cotton shirt, bought in the boys' department of a local store—or her denim jacket with its *Big Mac!* embossed buttons. Barbara McClintock did care about the esteem of her colleagues, however, and she died knowing how rich she was in that.

2

The Odd Member of the Family[1]

ALTHOUGH BARBARA MCCLINTOCK WAS A VERY pretty young woman with an active social life, she chose never to marry. From earliest childhood she knew she was destined to lead an unconventional life. She claimed that she preferred to be alone even before she knew how to walk. "My mother used to put a pillow on the floor and give me one toy and just leave me there. She said I didn't cry, didn't call for anything."[2]

Her parents had been youthful rebels themselves and had very untraditional views on childrearing. Even with such parents, whom she remembered as "wonderful," McClintock still marched to her own drummer. She later remembered, "I didn't belong to that family, but I'm glad I was in it. I was an odd member."[3]

She was born on June 16, 1902, in Hartford, Connecticut. Her parents already had two daughters, one a few months shy of four and one about two. Her mother was only 27, her father somewhat younger. The young parents were struggling to make their way in the world. The couple had married against the bride's family's wishes and could count on no financial help from her well-off family.

Barbara's mother, Sara Handy McClintock, was descended from two families that came to the New World in 1620 on the *Mayflower*. Brought up to excel at all the womanly arts, she was a skilled pianist, wrote pleasing verse, and painted with flair. Barbara's father, Thomas Henry McClintock, was the son of immigrants from the British Isles. Even though Thomas McClintock was soon to graduate from the Boston School of Medicine, Sara's father, Benjamin Handy, a Congregationalist minister, thought his daughter was too good for him. Despite her parents' disapproval, Sara and Thomas married. To cover Thomas's medical school debts, Sara used a small inheritance. To help the family make ends meet, she gave private piano lessons.

Eleanor Becomes Barbara

According to McClintock family lore, having already had two daughters, Sara and Thomas were eager for a boy. When a third daughter was born they named her Eleanor. By the time the infant was four months old, however, that name seemed too feminine for a child who showed unusual self-reliance. Although the change did not become official until 1943, when McClintock's father "legally had the name changed," the family dropped the name "Eleanor" for "Barbara."[4] That name seemed more forceful. In her thirties McClintock reported that "her father was so greatly disappointed that she was not a boy that he proceeded to raise her as a boy. Her got her boxing gloves when she was 4 years of age and as she came along she was provided with boys' toys and played boys' games."[5]

The arrival of this third daughter proved more than Sara McClintock could cope with, particularly after the birth of a fourth child—the much-desired boy—a year and a half later. From the time she was a toddler until it was time for her to start school, Barbara was sent to live with her father's sister and her husband for extended periods of time. Perhaps this method of coping with a difficult situation did not seem unusual to Sara McClintock. Her own mother had died while Sara was still an infant, and Sara had herself been raised by an aunt and uncle.

Away From Home

McClintock denied that she ever felt homesick while living with her aunt and uncle in Plymouth County, Massachusetts. She enjoyed accompanying her uncle, a fish dealer, on his daily rounds to the fish markets and from house to house in the country. When she first came to live with them, her uncle carried out his business in a horse and carriage. He later bought a motorized truck, and McClintock traced her early interest in cars to watching her uncle deal with his vehicle's frequent mechanical problems.

Barbara's interest in motors soon generalized to an interest in tools. She was disappointed when, after asking her father for a set, "he got tools that would fit in my hands, and I didn't think they were adequate. Though I didn't want to tell him that, they were not the tools I wanted. I wanted *real* tools, not tools for children."[6] Despite his failure to understand the true nature of her wish in this instance, however, Barbara in general admired her father for being "very perceptive with children."[7]

A Brooklyn Schoolgirl

In 1908 the McClintock family moved to Flatbush, a neighborhood in Brooklyn. Ten years earlier Brooklyn had become one of the five boroughs that make up New York City. The McClintocks were now well off enough to spend summers on Long Beach, Long Island. The improvement in the family's material status, however, did not lead to a warming of the relationship between Barbara and her mother. When her mother tried to hug her, Barbara pushed her away with a firm "no."

Sara McClintock never really knew what to make of this child of hers. She worried about Barbara's natural inclination for sitting by herself, either reading or absorbed in silent thought. Despite Barbara's obvious musical talent, Sara stopped giving Barbara piano lessons because she thought her daughter's dedication to practicing was too intense for her own good.

Yet in many ways, at least during McClintock's childhood, both parents honored her unconventional wishes. These former rebels were convinced that formal education was only one path to individual success. When Barbara formed a strong aversion to one of her teachers, they allowed her to stay home from school. When she developed a passion for ice skating, on days when the weather was ideal, they sent her off not to school but rather to Prospect Park, dressed in the finest skates and skating outfit. Respecting her love of sports and tree-climbing, at Barbara's request they had matching bloomers made for her dresses so that she could engage in rough-and-tumble and hang upside down without fear of having her underwear show.

One day Barbara ran home upset after being summoned to the home of a neighborhood busybody, who had taken it upon herself to convince the child "that it was time that I learned to do the things that girls should be doing."[8] Sara McClintock immediately picked up the telephone and warned the neighbor to mind her own business.

Out of Place

Despite her parents' support, however, Barbara seems to have felt out of place in the company of both boys and girls. On the one hand, "I didn't play with girls because they didn't play the way I did." On the other, she felt "only *tolerated* by the boys." As a result, she felt forced back on her own company. "So you couldn't win . . . you had to be alone. You couldn't be in a society you didn't belong to."[9] She began to understand "that I just had to make these adjustments to the fact that I was a girl doing the kinds of things that girls were not supposed to do."[10]

An Outstanding Student

Like her sisters before her, McClintock was an outstanding high school student. At Erasmus Hall High School she developed an interest in science and mathematics. After a teacher presented one method for solving problems, she discovered that she could develop alternative ways to arrive at the correct solution. "I would ask the instructor, 'Please, let me . . . see if I can't find the standard answer' and I'd find it. It was a tremendous joy, the whole process of finding that answer, just pure joy."[11]

By the time Barbara had completed high school, she had already accepted the fact that, for better or for worse, she was not a run-of-the-mill person. She was prepared to "take the consequences for the sake of an activity that I knew would give me great pleasure . . . . Whatever the consequences, *I had to go in that direction*."[12] When she graduated from Erasmus Hall, there would be a decisive struggle with her mother that would determine the rest of her life.

The Struggle to go to College

Sara McClintock had not found it hard to support her adolescent daughter's somewhat unconventional interest in sports. She balked, however, at the thought that Barbara's interest in science might lead her into a career as a college professor. Sara McClintock believed that only "a strange person, a person that didn't belong to society" would choose such a career.[13] She had already succeeded in talking her oldest daughter out of accepting a scholarship at Vassar College. Both of McClintock's older sisters married and settled down to more conventional lives. In Barbara's case, however, Sara McClintock succeeded only in postponing Barbara's dream of going to the College of Agriculture at Cornell University in Ithaca, in upstate New York. Sara's objections had nothing to do with money, since as a resident of New York State, Barbara would be entitled to enroll at the so-called Ag. School for free. Her objections had everything to do with the fate of unmarriageability that she was sure a college education would confer on Barbara.

College Dreams

Barbara graduated high school at the end of 1918, a semester early. At the time her father was not at home to support his third daughter's wishes. The United States had entered World War I in April 1917, and Dr. McClintock was sent to France as part of the army medical corps. McClintock later remembered that her father "sensed from the beginning that I would be going into graduate work."[14] Without her father's support, sixteen-year-old Barbara found herself incapable of overriding her mother's objections to her college plans. Determined nonetheless "to get the equivalent of a college education if I had to do it on my own," she spent the next six months working as an interviewer at an employment agency, and following a self-imposed course of reading at the public library in her spare time.[15]

Before the start of the fall semester in 1919, Barbara's father returned from Europe. Happily, he remained Barbara's advocate. She later remembered with deep gratitude that a college education became available to her "because I had the support of my father, the complete support. My mother—if she could have done it without raising trouble—she'd have stopped it."[16]

Far from stopping it, however, "once the decision was made," Sara McClintock moved heaven and earth to secure Barbara's admission in a few days' time to Cornell.[17] Taking the initiative, Sara called someone they knew who went to Cornell and learned that students whose names began with M were to register the following Tuesday at 8 a.m. She then presented herself at Erasmus Hall High School in search of whatever paperwork Barbara would need for registration. She came back empty-handed.

Not Giving Up

Undeterred, seventeen-year-old Barbara, who had been practicing self-reliance from infancy on, took the train to Ithaca on Monday and found a room to spend the night. The following morning, standing in line at the registrar's office with the other Ms, she realized that only she had no official documents to present to justify her admission to the Ag. School.

When her turn came the registrar scolded her: "You haven't got anything. How do you expect to get in?" As she later recalled, "just at that moment my name was called out in the room, loud enough for both of us to hear." The registrar excused himself for a moment, and when he returned, he gave her the papers that enabled her to register.

McClintock never knew just who intervened on her behalf, but she didn't care. "All I cared about was that I was in."[18] She would soon consider Ithaca, New York, and Cornell University more her permanent home than Brooklyn ever was.

3
The Three M's of Genetics

BARBARA MCCLINTOCK BEGAN HER COLLEGE career in 1919. As a slightly older geneticist would later write, that "was near enough to the beginnings of the modern phase of genetics so that one could easily look back to the time before Mendel's work was rediscovered."[1]

In her Nobel lecture, on December 8, 1983, Barbara McClintock echoed that thought: "Because I became actively involved in the subject of genetics only twenty-one years after the rediscovery, in 1900, of Mendel's principles of heredity, and at a stage when acceptance of these principles was not general among biologists, I have had the pleasure of witnessing and experiencing the excitement created by revolutionary changes in genetic concepts that have occurred over the past sixty-odd years."[2] She was too modest to add what one of her younger colleagues later pointed out: "this woman . . . lived through everything that had ever happened in our discipline except for Mendel; what she did not herself discover, she learned as it happened."[3]

Nor did McClintock compare herself to Mendel, although others certainly did. When announcing the Nobel Prize in 1983, the Karolinska Institute in Stockholm said, "The discovery of mobile genetic elements by McClintock is of profound importance for our understanding of the organization and function of genes." The institute, which has the responsibility of selecting the laureates for the Nobel Prize in the fields of physiology or medicine, also pointed out the uncanny similarity between the experience of that year's winner and of the founder of genetics himself, Gregor Mendel. As a contemporary news article summarized it, "Both were so far ahead of their time that their discoveries were not appreciated until the principles were rediscovered by other geneticists decades later."[4]

The so-called Father of Genetics, Mendel (1822–1884) was a monk and botanist who worked in Brno, in what is today the Czech Republic. Over a period of years he experimented with peas in the monastery garden. He studied how seven easily identifiable traits, including color, texture, and size, were passed down from generation to generation of pea plants. At the time people believed that offspring had traits that were a simple blend of the parents' traits. A younger colleague of McClintock's later described this belief: "In . . . Mendel's time, the mechanics of inheritance were not well understood. Most people in the nineteenth century thought of it as a blending of traits, like a mixing of water and wine or two colors of paint. What Mendel found was far from blending . . . ."[5]

Indeed, on the basis of his experiments, Mendel came to a radically different understanding of how characteristics or traits are handed down. After testing thousands of pea plants, he concluded that the egg cell of the female parent and the sperm cell of the male parent contain "factors" that control heredity. In 1909 these factors were named "genes." Mendel also concluded that every characteristic could appear in alternate forms. A pea's color might be yellow or it might be green, for example, and its texture might be smooth or it might be wrinkled.

According to Mendel, every plant receives two hereditary factors for each trait, one from each of its parents. The two possible forms of each trait may not contribute equally to the appearance of the trait in the offspring. One form of the trait will be dominant and the other recessive. The trait of the dominant form will determine the appearance of the offspring plant. Mendel determined that the trait for smooth seeds is dominant, while the trait for wrinkled seeds is recessive. Therefore, if an offspring inherits one gene for smooth seeds and one for wrinkled seeds, its seeds will be smooth. If, however, the offspring inherited from each parent the recessive gene for wrinkled seeds, its seeds would be wrinkled. Similarly, Mendel determined that for color, yellow was dominant over green.

Mendel's methods were as revolutionary as the conclusions he reached using them. He was the first to make the study of heredity into a mathematical science. Before his time no one had thought of testing thousands of plants under carefully controlled conditions. He cultivated the plants with great care and limited the number of traits he studied. These decisions enabled him to analyze his results with mathematical statistics. In turn, his statistical methods enabled him to derive laws from his many observations.

Although Mendel published his results in 1866, they became widely known only in 1900. In that year several different European scientists independently rediscovered his work. In the 19 years before Barbara McClintock arrived in Ithaca, New York, as a first-year student, Mendel's work also took root in the United States. In 1906 the new science based on Mendel's work was first called "genetics."

Emerson and Maize Genetics

In 1902 Rollins Adams Emerson (1873-1947), then a professor at the University of Nebraska, published his first paper incorporating Mendel's ideas. A dozen years later Emerson left Nebraska to become director of the plant breeding department at Cornell University's College of Agriculture. By that time Emerson had become a specialist in corn genetics. (In his attempt to determine whether the rules he found for heredity in peas applied to other organisms, Mendel himself had studied the genetics of corn.) Within a decade Barbara McClintock would become one of the most talented students in what Emerson transformed into a leading

Gregor Mendel, father of the scientific field of genetics.

center for corn genetics. As one of McClintock's closest lifetime colleagues, Marcus M. Rhoades, later said, "It is generally acknowledged that Emerson was the spiritual father of maize genetics . . . . He was the dominant figure among maize geneticists until the advent of cytogenetics and Barbara McClintock."[6]

Corn, or maize, had certain advantages as an experimental plant for geneticists. Each of the many kernels on a cob of corn results from a separate mating of egg and sperm. Since each corn cob contains many offspring from many matings, a scientist's chances of reaching conclusions that have statistical significance are good. Another advantage is that the egg and the sperm cells are conveniently packaged and easily separable. The tassel or flowering part at the top of the stalk is the male reproductive structure. In the middle of the stalk is the ear, the female reproductive structure. The ear—the cob and its rows of kernels—is protected by husks, special leaves. Long, threadlike silks that extend beyond the tips of the protective husks capture pollen, tiny grains produced in the male organs. Ordinarily, the wind carries corn pollen among nearby plants in the field. A maize geneticist who wishes to control the spread of pollen, however, can do so by covering the tassels and silks with paper bags and then brushing pollen from a designated male parent onto selected silks.

Another reason why geneticists found corn a useful organism to study is that it is easy to pick out genetic mutations on an ear of corn. A mutation is a permanent change in the hereditary material of cells that causes a change in certain traits. Changes in the color of corn kernels result from mutations. As one writer puts it, "The variegated colors of [corn's] kernels functioned like a technicolor spread sheet of genetic data; genetic changes were as plain as the kernels on the cob."[7] (A spread sheet is a worksheet on which a variety of related topics are organized in columns for easy reference and comparison.) Early in the 1900s Emerson figured out that an unusual mutation caused alternating streaks of colored and uncolored cells in some varieties of Indian corn. What caused the mutation, however, was a mystery that would be solved only years later. The solution lay in McClintock's theory of mobile genetic elements.

Morgan and Fruit Fly Genetics

Corn was thus a popular organism for geneticists to study, but it was not the only one. Another popular experimental organism was the fruit fly. Since these insects are attracted to decaying fruit and vegetables, they are easy to obtain. Their size, color markings, and patterns of bristles make it simple to distinguish between the two sexes. They reproduce in a little over a week, and each mating yields hundreds of offspring. Corn, by contrast, has only one growing season per year (although in the subtropics or in a greenhouse it can have two). Because fruit flies produced so many offspring, they provided geneticists an opportunity to screen many thousands of flies for new mutations. These mutations could then be followed through many generations because of the rapid life cycle of fruit flies.

While R. A. Emerson was establishing himself as a leading corn geneticist, Thomas Hunt Morgan (1866–1945), at Columbia University, was earning a reputation based on his work with fruit flies. Morgan demonstrated that each Mendelian gene had a specific position along a chromosome. (Chromosomes had been named and described in 1881 by a cytologist who studied them under a microscope. They were the bodies that absorbed color—the meaning of the Greek "chrom"—when the cells were treated with dye.) Each chromosome could be mapped to show which genes lay on it. Having found that certain genes were linked together on a single chromosome, Morgan was able to explain why there could be more genes than chromosomes. For his greatest achievement, the chromosome theory of heredity, Morgan was awarded the Nobel Prize for physiology or medicine in 1933, exactly a half-century before McClintock was awarded the same prize.

When Barbara McClintock enrolled at Cornell in autumn 1919, who could have known that she would one day win the Thomas Hunt Morgan Medal of the Genetics Society of America, as she did in June 1981? Who could have predicted that one of her "jumping genes" would eventually be found to cause the wrinkled seeds in some of Mendel's peas, as happened in 1990? And who could have foreseen that McClintock's importance to the field of genetics would be summarized thus by another of its giants in the year before her death: "There are really three main figures in the history of genetics. The three M's: Mendel, Morgan, and McClintock. Gregor Mendel and Thomas Hunt Morgan showed us how regular the genome is, and Barbara McClintock showed us how irregular it is."[8]

4 The Golden Age of Maize Cytogenetics at Cornell[1]

MCCLINTOCK WAS NEITHER THE FIRST NOR the only woman to thrive at Cornell. According to a history of women at that university, Cornell was "a notable pioneer in women's education." It was not only "the first major institution in the eastern United States to admit women along with men (1872)" but also the first "to award the Doctor of Science degree to a woman in the United States (1895)."[2] Among the distinguished women graduates of Cornell before McClintock were those who went on to leadership careers in medicine, women's rights, civil engineering, and law. One "of the few institutions training women to a high level of proficiency in the sciences," Cornell also "ranked among the leading institutions which awarded doctorates to outstanding women in science before 1920."[3]

More than fifty years after completing her undergraduate education, McClintock recalled loving the experience. "I was entranced at the very first lecture I went to. It was zoology, and I was just completely entranced. I was doing now what I really wanted to do, and I never lost that joy all the way through college."[4] The professor for the course, Hugh Daniel Reed, was also the chairman of Cornell's zoology department. Reed's was the first complete course at Cornell in the subject, which deals with the study of animals.[5]

Over the course of her undergraduate career McClintock sampled a wide variety of courses, officially dropping out of those that failed to live up to her expectations.

She did not excel at every course. In fact, she failed a music class she took her freshman year. In her second attempt at music, she earned a C+. That course, she later recalled, "stood me in good stead when I was in my senior year in college and used to play in a little jazz combo."[6] Many years later McClintock told a younger colleague how much she had enjoyed playing with that "banjo band." She remembered driving the members of the band and their instruments, packed into her Model T Ford, to their gigs. She also "enjoyed being part of a musical group, harmonizing with the others and playing along with them."[7]

McClintock gave up her involvement with the combo by the end of her first year in graduate school. A performer's late nights left her too groggy during the day to concentrate on her real passion: botany—the study of plants. She remained a music lover for the rest of her life, however. Others would recall "her splendid phonograph" and "how much

McClintock enjoyed music and how well she could whistle and play the accordion."[8]

At Cornell McClintock found, perhaps to her surprise, that she was very much in demand socially. She was elected president of the women's freshman class and was asked to join a sorority. None of the Jewish girls to whom she was drawn "because they were quite different from the rest of the population at Cornell" were welcome in the sorority, however. When McClintock became aware of their exclusion, "I thought about it for a while, and broke my pledge. . . . I just couldn't stand that kind of discrimination."[9] McClintock was not interested in belonging to any such group herself.

During her first two years she also dated widely. Finding herself attracted to artistic types, rather than scientists, she would recall decades later that the relationships were "not casual involvements." She felt a "strong emotional attachment" more than once.[10] Later, as a graduate student, she had a steady relationship with her undergraduate chemistry instructor. Finally she broke the relationship off. She had decided that "marriage would have been a disaster. Men weren't strong enough . . . and I knew I was a dominant person . . . . I knew that I'd become very intolerant, that I'd make their lives miserable."[11]

McClintock remembered being something of a trend-setter on the campus. During the "roaring twenties," when many women went in for unconventional dress and behavior, short women's haircuts soon became popular. McClintock later claimed that in 1920, when she talked an Ithaca barber into lopping off her hair, she became the first woman at Cornell to wear a "bob." Whether or not this memory was accurate, however, is not clear.

When McClintock was awarded the Nobel Prize in 1983, she was asked to submit an autobiographical statement. The events she covered in that essay were those she considered "by far, the most influential in directing my scientific life." The opening sentence focuses on what she clearly considered one of the most important courses of her college career: "In the fall of 1921 I attended the only course in genetics open to undergraduate students at Cornell University. It was conducted by C. B. Hutchison, then a professor in the Department of Plant Breeding, College of Agriculture."[12]

Barbara McClintock's college yearbook portrait.

In the autobiographical statement, McClintock singled out two other courses that led her to a career in cytogenetics. Although Hutchison himself left Cornell to direct the Agriculture Farm at the University of California at Davis, he wanted to make sure that McClintock continued to study genetics. "When the undergraduate genetics course was completed in January 1922, I received a telephone call from Dr. Hutchison.

He must have sensed my intense interest in the content of his course because the purpose of his call was to invite me to participate in the only other genetics course given at Cornell. It was scheduled for graduate students . . . . Obviously, this telephone call cast the die for my future. I remained with genetics thereafter."[13]

Students who enrolled in this graduate-level course, taught by Hutchison's former assistant, were supposed to have completed the course in cytology taught by Lester Whyland Sharp. McClintock "enrolled in both courses simultaneously."[14] Having taken these courses, McClintock "had no doubts about the direction I wished to follow for an advanced degree. It would involve chromosomes and their genetic content and expressions, in short, cytogenetics."[15]

Early Discoveries

McClintock completed the requirements for her undergraduate diploma a semester early, just as she had for her high school diploma. In a letter to the Dean of the Graduate School in February 1923, Professor Sharp recommended that McClintock be admitted to the doctoral program at the College of Agriculture. Having been "permitted to register grad," she signed up to major in cytology under Sharp's direction, with minors in genetics and zoology.[16] There is no record that McClintock applied to major in genetics, which was taught in the Plant Breeding Department. Professor Emerson, the head of the corn genetics program at Cornell, welcomed women to enroll as graduate students in that department. Perhaps he advised McClintock not to, however, thinking that she would have an easier time finding a job with a Ph.D. degree from the Botany Department, where Sharp was employed.[17] McClintock was awarded the Cornell graduate scholarship for botany, which supported her during her first year as a graduate student.

Social life was important to McClintock as a graduate student, but her circle seems to have included mainly others in related fields. She was actively involved in the student-faculty club organized by the Plant Breeding Department. This organization was called the Synapsis Club after a term from cell biology. During the process of synapsis, chromosomes from each parent pair up. Both the Synapsis Club and its offshoot, the Razzberry Club, promoted other kinds of pairings as well. The scientific friendships that formed in the process of the club's regular dinner meetings, seminars, and outings resulted in some romantic relationships and even some marriages.[18]

McClintock, however, was more interested in a different union: "the exciting and novel marriage of maize cytology and genetics that was occurring at Cornell."[19] In the fall of 1924, her second year of graduate work, McClintock was hired to assist cytologist Lowell F. Randolph. A recent Ph.D. student of Sharp's, Randolph had been the teaching assistant in the cytology course McClintock took in her junior year. In

February 1926 Randolph and McClintock published a paper on the cytology of an unusual maize plant that she had discovered the previous summer while working in the Plant Breeding Garden—the several-acre experimental field where Cornell's maize scientists grew their plants.[20] This unusual plant, called a triploid, had three sets of chromosomes rather than the normal two sets.

The relationship between Randolph and McClintock did not flourish, however. She was resentful that his name appeared first on the paper, when she believed she had done most of the work.[21] Marcus M. Rhoades had not yet arrived at Cornell when the rupture between Randolph and McClintock occurred. Many years later, Rhoades, by then McClintock's longtime colleague and friend, described the outcome of the short-lived collaboration: "Their brief association was momentous because it led to the birth of maize cytogenetics."[22]

In February 1925, before discovering the triploid plant, McClintock was awarded her master's degree and began working toward her doctorate. Her master's thesis reviewed previous research on different types of cereals, especially wheat. Finding the triploid maize plant that summer shifted the focus of her research. Over the next several years, she made use of it to accomplish what no one had yet succeeded in doing: distinguishing each of the corn chromosomes from one another, counting them, and identifying the linked genes that resided on different chromosomes. Improving on a recently developed technique for making microscope slides and staining chromosomes that Randolph had taught her, she succeeded where he had failed. In March 1929 McClintock's paper based on her doctoral work was published. In June 1929 further work led her to find and number the ten corn chromosomes, each one of which she associated with a distinct set of physical traits. She thus played the leading role in assigning to the different chromosomes the sets of genes that were transmitted as a group.[23]

Forming Lifelong Professional Ties

After receiving her doctorate in June 1927, McClintock was immediately hired as an instructor in the botany department at Cornell. At that time the position of instructor was the first step on the road to an appointment as a professor. Cornell, however, was in bad financial shape. It was hard for anyone, male or female, to get a secure position there. The most gifted graduates were encouraged to apply for postdoctoral fellowships elsewhere. Indeed, Emerson, who had been appointed dean of the graduate school in 1925, had recommended McClintock for a fellowship to study abroad, but her application was turned down. The International Education Board, which sponsored the fellowship, expressed concerns that "the applicant is a woman and may leave the field of science at any time."[24]

McClintock's failure to win that fellowship turned out to be a blessing in disguise. Her presence at Cornell over the next several years made possible what others later called "the golden age of maize cytogenetics." According to a recent assessment of McClintock's contribution to that effort, "Her cytological breakthroughs brought previously invisible objects and phenomena to light."[25]

As McClintock noted in her Nobel autobiography, between the time she completed her Ph.D. requirements and the completion of "studies aimed at associating each of the ten chromosomes comprising the maize complement with the genes each carries," a number of other talented scientists arrived at Cornell. These included George Beadle, Marcus Rhoades, Charles Burnham, and Harriet Creighton. The newcomers joined McClintock to form "a close-knit group eager to discuss all phases of genetics, including those being revealed or suggested by our own efforts."[26]

Opportunities for this group to bond together existed both in the Plant Breeding Garden and at their cubbies—the cubicles where they worked in crowded conditions in the Agricultural College's Stone Hall. Harriet Creighton later described how the overcrowding actually enhanced their education: "How could this jammed-up inadequate arrangement be of benefit to anyone? Because, when any one of us working on corn found anything puzzling or exciting on a microscope slide, every one could come immediately to look. Interpretations could be launched and argued and thinking could certainly be stimulated. The excitement of seeing what someone else had found carried each of us over the times when we were not turning up anything new. All of us profited from the quick, easy, and open exchange of observations and interpretations."[27]

Similarly, in the Plant Breeding Garden, while each young scientist had a specific plot to cultivate, the group as a whole shared the hard work of planting and tending the corn.[28] During pollination season, for example, all the corn scientists, including Emerson, worked a seven-day week together. In that informal setting, Emerson did most of his teaching during lunch and rest breaks. Shaped by his "ethical and cooperative spirit," the students eventually grew into "an expanded network of maize researchers who freely shared their materials and unpublished research, thus resulting in rapid progress in fundamental genetic research."[29]

Emerson recognized that he had an exceptional group of students working with him. In January 1930 he wrote, "Beadle and Rhoades and also Dr. Burnham went to McClintock who was willing to spend any amount of time in helping them with the cytological aspects of their problems. These three men with McClintock's help have turned up more interesting and important things the past season [corn growing season 1929] than usually come to light in several years."[30]

In her Nobel autobiography McClintock returned the compliment. She credited Emerson for encouraging these budding scientists and for overlooking "some of our seemingly strange behaviors." She also noted that the ties the young scientists forged at Cornell in the

1920s and early 1930s remained strong over the years. "The communal experience profoundly affected each one of us."[31] Recollecting that period from his own perspective many decades later, Rhoades confirmed that "The years at Cornell from 1928 to 1935 were ones of intense cytogenetical activity. Progress was rapid, the air electric."[32]

A Landmark Paper, But No Permanent Job

McClintock's reputation as a leader in the field was secured as a result of the research project she collaborated on with Harriet Creighton. Creighton, who had just received an undergraduate degree from Wellesley College, arrived at Cornell in the summer of 1929. Seven years younger than McClintock, Creighton admired her older friend for "the conviction that always you gave full physical and mental effort to whatever pursuit you cared about."[33] Decades later she remembered McClintock's attention to her corn plants during a torrential rainstorm. While all the members of the maize group "had genetic stocks that were distinctive and the basis of our research," McClintock alone arrived at the Plant Breeding Garden "long before dawn to save her plants. If she lost them, she would have blamed only herself . . . for not having made the maximum effort to save her research."[34] Creighton also remembered McClintock as a formidable opponent on the tennis

McClintock studies and records her observations in a corn field.

courts, where they met at 5 p.m. when the weather permitted.

In the spring of 1930 McClintock suggested that Creighton collaborate with her on the important problem of "crossing-over." Geneticists believed that chromosomes not only carried genes but also exchanged genetic information during cell division. No one had yet provided cytological proof to confirm that belief, however. Using a special strain of corn McClintock had bred, the two women were the first to publish proof that chromosomes physically exchange parts during cell division. Creighton wrote up the crossing-over experiment as part of her doctoral thesis. In the thesis she expressed her "indebtedness to Dr. Barbara McClintock for her aid and constant encouragement during the course of this study, which she suggested."[35]

When McClintock suggested they collaborate on the crossing-over experiment, the inexperienced Creighton did not fully understand its significance.[36] She had to be encouraged to publish the paper with what she considered meager results. Famed geneticist Thomas Hunt Morgan learned about the results of McClintock's and Creighton's research while delivering a series of lectures at Cornell in spring 1931. He urged the young women to submit their work for publication. Perhaps motivated by Morgan's visit, Professor Emerson, whom the corn group at Cornell called "Chief," sent their article to the *Proceedings of the National Academy of Sciences*. The paper appeared in that prestigious journal in 1931, preceded by another paper by McClintock alone. Years later the joint article was included in a book called *Classic Papers in Genetics*. In his preface to the article, the editor of that book wrote, "This paper has been called a landmark in experimental genetics. It is more than that—it is a cornerstone."[37]

The publication of the crossing-over paper made McClintock famous among geneticists worldwide. Not yet thirty years old, she was acknowledged as "a leader in the corn genetics community and the preeminent corn cytogeneticist."[38] This acclaim, however, did not guarantee her a job. By the time the paper appeared, the United States was in the tight grip of the Great Depression. This economic crisis began with the crash of the stock market in October 1929 and lasted through the 1930s. Neither McClintock nor her male colleagues in the Cornell corn group had an easy time finding permanent positions. As one McClintock biographer put it, "None of the stellar trio of McClintock, Beadle, and Rhoades obtained permanent jobs right out of their doctoral program."[39] When she finally gave up her instructorship at Cornell at the end of June 1931, it was for the first in a series of research fellowships.

On and off throughout the early 1930s McClintock continued to return to Cornell for research stints. Even after August 1936, when her last extended stay there ended, her ties with Cornell remained unsevered. She never was offered a regular professorial position at her alma mater, but she was one of a select group invited to participate in a new Professor-at-Large program there from 1965 to 1974. More than a decade after her death, her name still carries weight at Cornell. As of February 2004, there were two Barbara McClintock Professors at the university. Cornell appoints to these prestigious professorships faculty members whose pioneering research in plant biology or genetics promises to open new areas of discovery, just as McClintock's continues to do.[40]

5

Fellowships at Home and Abroad

IT WAS NOT AN EASY THING FOR ANY SCIENTIST to secure a National Research Council Fellowship or a Guggenheim Memorial Foundation Fellowship in the 1930s. It was an even harder thing for a woman scientist to win one of these coveted fellowships. Barbara McClintock was one of a few to win both.[1]

In 1919 the Rockefeller Foundation of New York, a giant philanthropic organization, created the National Research Council Fellowships to provide a year or two of support to young scientists who had already completed their doctorates. These NRC fellowships helped some of the most promising scientists advance their careers. They could continue their research while they looked around for permanent positions. In 1923 the NRC included plant scientists among the group eligible for fellowships. Over the next fifteen years, 86 botanists received NRC fellowships. Only five of those were women. From 1931 to 1933, Barbara McClintock's NRC fellowship supported her work at the University of Missouri, and the California Institute of Technology (popularly known as Caltech). Cornell remained McClintock's home institution, but no NRC funds went to Cornell.[2]

In 1947 McClintock was honored with the Achievement Award of the American Association of University Women. In accepting the award, McClintock recognized the role her NRC fellowship had played in transforming her into a candidate for awards like the one she was being honored with that day. It had provided her and other young scientists with the opportunity "to do something where you wanted to, when you wanted to, no restrictions, no obligations, you could work all night if you wanted. You did not have to get up and teach the next morning. To do what you wanted and really have a wonderful time doing it."[3] The freedom to focus exclusively on her research was clearly something McClintock valued highly.

McClintock began her NRC fellowship with a summer at the University of Missouri. She had been invited there by Lewis J. Stadler. Some years earlier Stadler had gone to Cornell in hopes of earning a Ph.D. with Rollins A. Emerson. As McClintock's colleague Marcus Rhoades described it, however, Stadler "left after a few months, having made a poor impression on the plant breeding faculty."[4] Determined to become a corn geneticist all the same, Stadler returned to Missouri, where he had previously earned his master's degree, and succeeded in earning his doctorate there. Stadler's success did not go unnoticed. In mid-1926 he returned to Cornell to work with

Emerson as a National Research Council Fellow. During his time at Cornell, Stadler was one of many graduate students and postdoctoral fellows whom Sharp sent to McClintock "for advice and consultation on their research."[5] By 1931 Stadler had become a major figure in the field and a pioneer in using X-rays to create mutations in corn. When he needed help in analyzing their cytology, he knew where to turn. As McClintock explained decades later in her Nobel lecture, "By the summer of 1931 Stadler had many plants in his field at Columbia, Missouri," which he had exposed to X-rays. "Stadler had asked me if I would be willing to examine such plants . . . . I was delighted to do so, as this would be a very new experience."[6]

In her Nobel lecture McClintock traced her later discovery of "jumping genes" to her early examinations that summer at Stadler's lab of the behavior of broken chromosome ends. She noticed that bombarding corn kernels with X-rays often caused chromosomes to break. She soon determined that there was something special about the tips of chromosomes. A broken chromosome end might fuse with another broken end, while an unbroken tip would not. When broken chromosome ends fused together, they formed a ring. Soon she would write a paper establishing that ring-shaped chromosomes played a role in variegated corn, whose kernels—with patches or spots of different color—varied in appearance. By the end of the 1930s the end portions of chromosomes were called "telomeres," from the Greek words for "end" and "segment." McClintock's early work on telomeres opened up a field of research that continues to thrive in the twenty-first century.

McClintock spent the bulk of her two-year NRC fellowship at Caltech in Pasadena, California, not far from Los Angeles. Thomas Hunt Morgan had left behind his "fly room" at Columbia in 1928 to head a new genetics group at this up-and-coming technical university. One of the ways Morgan transformed his fledgling department into a world center for genetics research was by bringing young talent in from other institutions for short periods of time. Among the young people who spent time with Morgan at Caltech was McClintock's close Cornell friend and colleague George Beadle.

Unlike Cornell, which from its founding had stressed the importance of educating women, Caltech's community at the time (and for many years to come) was not friendly to women. In 1931, as the first woman postdoctoral fellow at Caltech, McClintock stuck out in more ways than one. On one hand, she was the only researcher in the otherwise "disappointing" group there to impress the director of the natural sciences division of the Rockefeller Foundation on a visit to Pasadena. She alone seemed to him to be "quite first class."[7] On the other hand, she also experienced some discrimination. One day faculty member Sterling Emerson invited her to lunch at the Athenaeum, Caltech's faculty club. Years later McClintock would remember the meal as something of an ordeal, with all eyes focused on her as she was ushered into the dining room.[8]

McClintock did not let the discrimination ruin her time at Caltech. She managed both to do significant work there and to have a circle of friends. She played enough tennis to give herself "a nice flat foot from playing on those hard courts."[9] The time she spent with George Beadle and his wife, Marion, led to an amusing run-in with the law. The three friends were driving in town one day in McClintock's Model A Ford, a two-seater. Marion Beadle was at the driver's wheel, McClintock in the passenger seat, and Beadle perched on the running board, a small ledge beneath the car door. In Pasadena it was illegal to drive with someone hanging on there, partly because that person might obscure the driver's view. The party of three were duly stopped by a cop. As the officer began to write the ticket, McClintock talked him out of doing so by saying, "Don't worry, that's her husband, she can see right through him."[10]

Among those who remembered McClintock's "wry, dry sense of humor" was one of her friends from her third-floor lab in the Kerckhoff biology building. Graduate student James Bonner, who later went on to become a professor of biology at Caltech, recalled that although they spoke mostly about corn genetics, fruit flies, and other geneticists, "we had long discussions about . . . everything else during the evenings."[11] McClintock explained to Bonner why she intended to remain single: She had met only two men—both geneticists—whom she could even imagine as husbands, and neither of them was available. In any case, McClintock's lack of romantic involvement did not stop her from participating in the department social life, which, as Bonner recalled, included parties at faculty homes and trips to nearby beaches, mountains, and deserts.

Most of the time at Caltech, as elsewhere, McClintock was focused on her work, not her social life. Her experiments at Caltech led up to another major discovery on her part. She identified what became called the nucleolar-organizing region (NOR) or nucleolus organizer (NO). This region of the chromosome contains the ribosomal RNA genes and associated proteins necessary for the synthesis of proteins in the cell.

Unhappy Guggenheim Fellow In Nazi Germany

By early 1933 McClintock had accomplished a great deal of important work as an NRC fellow. She had also lined up her next prestigious fellowship, a Guggenheim. These postdoctoral fellowships were established in 1925 by the John Simon Guggenheim Memorial Foundation. Over the next decade 144 scientists were awarded Guggenheim fellowships. Only five of those scientists were women, and Barbara McClintock was one of that select group.[12] As part of her application for the Guggenheim, she submitted letters of recommendation from Emerson and Sharp at

Cornell, Stadler at Missouri, and Morgan at Caltech. Her intention was to spend a year in Germany at the Kaiser Wilhelm Institute for Biology, which had been the home institution of Curt Stern.[13]

Stern was a fruit-fly geneticist who had spent some time in the 1920s at Columbia with Morgan's group. Back in Germany in 1931, he had been studying fly chromosomes in search of proof to the same problem—"crossing-over"—that McClintock and Creighton had approached through a study of corn chromosomes. Years later Stern remembered with some amusement that when it came time for him to present his results at an important colloquium, he was totally ignorant of the fact that the two women corn geneticists at Cornell had "scooped" him by publishing their cytogenetic data first: "I gave my paper with the enthusiasm of a successful youth. Soon after, one of my colleagues from the Kaiser Wilhelm Institute came to me and said: 'I didn't want to spoil your fun but while you were on vacation a paper came out written by Harriet Creighton and Barbara McClintock who did experiments in maize equivalent to what you just announced as unique.' May I confess . . . that I am still grateful to my colleague for permitting the feeling of triumph for half an hour longer than I would have had if he had told me about the Creighton-McClintock paper *before* my talk."[14]

Stern was among the gifted young geneticists who spent a year at Caltech in 1932, where McClintock became close with him and his wife, Evelyn. Stern did not return as planned to his home institution in Berlin, however. In January 1933 the Nazi party took over the German government. An important part of the Nazi platform was the elimination of Jews from German life. When Stern, a Jew himself, learned that Jews were being removed from their teaching and research positions in Germany, he decided to stay in the United States. He would spend his career at American universities.

In March 1933 McClintock wrote Stern to tell him of her "good news": "I got a telegram last night . . . stating that I got the Guggenheim fellowship . . . . I think, therefore, that I am all set for another year and pleasantly so . . . . I applied to begin my fellowship in October. I shall probably see you then sometime in October."[15] Stern, however, would not return to Germany, and for other reasons, too, things did not turn out as "pleasantly" for her there as McClintock had hoped.

McClintock waited until her return to the United States to speak openly to the Sterns about what she encountered in Germany. In December 1934, about eight months after her return, she reported, "My experiences in Germany were not too happy. I was very discouraged when I returned and did not want to do much talking about it. I couldn't have picked a worse time. The general morale of the scientific worker was anything but encouraging. There were almost no students from other countries. The political situation and its devastating results were too prominent."[16]

McClintock's maize research required many long hours at work under the hot sun categorizing each ear of corn and taking precautions against accidental pollination.

In an earlier letter to the Sterns, written while she was still in Germany, she was more guarded about her reactions to what was going on in Germany: "My opinions and the general opinions I can best translate to you when I get home." She alluded, however, to the difficult situation confronting the family of another distinguished German-Jewish geneticist, Richard Goldschmidt.

But even the deteriorating political situation did not keep McClintock from offering in the same letter a humorous assessment to the Sterns of her German language skills: "The language has come very hard for me . . . . We Americans and English are all relatively stupid in languages . . . . It was something of a relief to me to find that I do not take the booby prize although I compete for it." McClintock also explained to the Sterns that in addition to everything else, she was physically ill in Berlin (the result of an overactive thyroid). She decided to spend a month at the "well-equipped" Botanical Institute in Freiburg, Germany, which she found "beautiful . . . and comfortable," but ended up not returning to Berlin. Instead, she planned to travel back to the States with a stop in Norwich, England, to visit the John Innes Institute, an important center of botanical science. Her letter to the Sterns from Freiburg concluded with several pieces of information: "I expect to be back in the middle of April. I am job hunting! The Guggenheim foundation is allowing their fellows to do work in the U.S. . . . I shall work in Ithaca this summer."[17]

A Research Assistant's Fears of Joblessness

McClintock's Guggenheim funding would run out in September 1934. For the next two years she managed to find other sources to support her work, but the fear of unemployment was never far from her mind. In 1934 Emerson received a grant from the Rockefeller Foundation for five years of support for his corn genetics group at Cornell. He managed to get additional funding to hire McClintock as his research assistant for a year and then for a second year.[18] Emerson gave McClintock the freedom to work on whatever research problems interested her.[19] She continued her cytological studies of X-rayed plants, advancing her understanding of how some chromosomes become shaped like rings.[20] Of course, no one knew at the time that this research would lead to the discovery that would win her a Nobel Prize. At the time the fear that she would never find a long-term suitable position was a very vivid force in McClintock's life.

A peek into the diary of the director of the natural sciences division at the Rockefeller Foundation sheds some light on McClintock's job prospects at Cornell: "The Department of Botany does not wish to reappoint her, chiefly because they realize that her interest is entirely in research and that she will leave Ithaca as soon as she can obtain suitable employment elsewhere; and partly because she is not entirely successful as a teacher of undergraduate work. The Botany Department obviously prefers a less gifted person who will be content to accept a large amount of routine duty. At present McClintock has absolutely nothing in sight for next year . . . . this situation will cause [her] so much worry that it may seriously interfere with her scientific work for a considerable period."[21]

A letter from McClintock nearly a year later confirmed that fears of future joblessness did affect her work. She knew that her funding for her position as Emerson's research assistant would soon run out. She wrote her old Cornell friend Charles Burnham in April 1935, "No sign of a job has turned up for me as yet. I cant [sic] say that it makes me feel very peppy to be still in the unemployed list although I am getting a decent salary just now. The uncertainty gets under my skin a bit and hinders my spirits. My work has suffered in consequence without the necessary stimulus."[22]

McClintock must have shared her job anxieties with her parents, because her father tried on his own to do something to help. In summer 1935 Dr. McClintock visited two Rockefeller administrators to see if the foundation could help find a permanent position for his daughter. In his notes on the visit and on a subsequent conversation with McClintock herself, one administrator made clear that "the decision to renew her [Cornell research assistantship] grant was made before her father's visit and in any event the visit could not have influenced our decision one way or the other."[23]

With or without her father's help, would McClintock ever find the right job?

6

From the Wrong Job to the Right One

IN THE SPRING OF 1936 MCCLINTOCK'S SEARCH for the right job finally seemed to have ended happily. The United States Department of Agriculture and the Rockefeller Foundation had agreed to fund a Regional Laboratory of Plant Genetics for Lewis Stadler at the University of Missouri. Stadler wrote, "Doctor McClintock is unquestionably the best cytologist who could have been appointed and is in my opinion unsurpassed in her field."[1] McClintock, who had begun her NRC fellowship five years earlier with Stadler's X-rayed plants in Columbia, Missouri, accepted Stadler's offer to join him there again. This time, however, as an assistant professor of botany, she would be a member of the faculty at the university.[2]

At first McClintock was energized by the work she accomplished there. She continued to examine chromosome breakage in plants, leading to her description in 1938 of what she called the "breakage–fusion–bridge" cycle. The discovery of this damage that some chromosomes sustained repeatedly was another feather in McClintock's already highly plumed geneticist's cap. Recognizing her growing importance in the field, the Genetics Society of America elected her vice president in 1939. (Six years later she would become the society's first woman president.) Soon the breakage–fusion–bridge cycle was linked to the symptoms of radiation sickness. After being exposed to very high doses of radioactivity—in a nuclear explosion, for example—people can die from radiation sickness.[3]

Her work was so satisfying that McClintock resented having to leave the lab in order to catch some rest. In the summer of 1940 she wrote Charles Burnham, "Have been working like hell on an exciting over-all problem in genetics with wonderful results. It gets me up early and puts me to bed late!"[4] Two months later she wrote again: "Just now I am finishing up a paper on broken chromosomes and then the ring chromosome material . . . comes next to be written up."[5]

Her enthusiasm for her research, however, did not carry over to her job in general. In the same October letter and in a letter the previous month, McClintock made clear to Burnham that the job at Missouri just wasn't the right one for her. In September she wrote, "I have decided that I must look for another job . . . . I dont [sic] mind going down in salary as money is'nt [sic] a factor . . . ."[6] Her October letter explained some of the reasons for her dissatisfaction: a university professor's burden, which includes "teaching . . . and graduate students," in addition to research, just didn't leave her with enough time to "do all three well enough and also try to keep up with the literature."[7]

There were other reasons leading McClintock to conclude that she could not stay at Missouri.[8] She and Stadler did not always see eye to eye. One researcher recalled often seeing McClintock leave Stadler's office "in tears."[9] McClintock realized, however, that if Stadler left Missouri she might be even worse off. When he considered taking a position at Caltech, the dean informed McClintock that her duties might change. McClintock understood that to mean that her teaching responsibilities might increase. She also did not get along with some of her colleagues, who may have resented her. A student at the time recalled that a woman professor of zoology lectured about the nucleolus for an hour "without even mentioning McClintock's brilliant paper on the organizer region!"[10] McClintock also resented the "constant exclusion" she felt as a woman at Missouri, as she had at Caltech.[11]

Perhaps more serious than such snubs from both male and female colleagues, McClintock never felt the university community accepted her unconventional behavior. One Sunday, for example, she arrived at her office without her keys, only to find the building locked. She was later taken to task for climbing through a window to gain entry. The dean thought she was a "trouble maker."[12]

Full-Time Researcher at the Carnegie Institution

In April 1941 McClintock requested a leave of absence to look for a position elsewhere. She wrote her friend and colleague Marcus Rhoades, "This job, regardless of permanent tenure, would certainly kill my vitality."[13] The following month the University of Missouri granted her a leave of absence, without pay, from September 1941 through August 1942. McClintock expected that if her job search proved unsuccessful she would return.

She had, in any case, been invited to spend the summer of 1941 as a visiting scientist at the Department of Genetics of the Carnegie Institution of Washington (CIW). This facility was located at Cold Spring Harbor, Long Island, New York. Marcus Rhoades, then at Columbia University, arranged an appointment for her as a guest investigator in the botany department there for the rest of her leave. McClintock accepted an invitation to return to the Department of Genetics at Cold Spring Harbor as a salaried guest investigator throughout 1942. Before that year was out, a full-time research position funded by CIW at Cold Spring Harbor was made available to her. McClintock officially resigned from the faculty at the University of Missouri that spring.

Over the years a story spread suggesting that McClintock left Missouri because she was denied tenure there as a woman. The story is exaggerated.[14] In March 1941 Stadler wrote Rhoades that McClintock was "definitely slated for a promotion this spring, and [the chairman of the botany department] has told her so . . . ."[15] When McClintock decided in 1942 to accept the full-time CIW research position at Cold Spring Harbor, the University of Missouri made her a counter offer, which she turned down. In 1954, after Lewis Stadler's death, the University of Missouri tried unsuccessfully to lure McClintock back to replace him as head of the genetics project. She preferred the life of a full-time researcher to the life of a professor. Others might have chosen differently. As she explained in a 1945 letter to her old friend and colleague George Beadle, "The goals I have aimed at can not be compared with the goals that many people are able to aim at . . . . The compensation lies in the fact that I am much freer to wander around and do the things I like to do without feeling that I must maintain a standard pattern of behavior."[16]

At the Carnegie Institution of Washington McClintock had finally found the right job. When steel magnate and philanthropist Andrew Carnegie founded the institution in 1902, he intended it as a scientific home for unusually imaginative and dedicated scientists who were likely to do cutting-edge research. When CIW president Vannevar Bush invited McClintock to do her genetics research at Cold Spring Harbor, he not only chose a scientist who would live up to Carnegie's ideals but also made it possible for McClintock to do so. As a younger colleague of McClintock commented years after McClintock's death, the position at Carnegie gave

McClintock the opportunity to turn her back on "the ordinary academic world, with its routine of committees, teaching and other kinds of busy-ness," and to focus full-time on her science.[17]

McClintock herself did not realize immediately just how good the fit was between her and the Carnegie Institution of Washington. She later reflected on how long it took for her to come to this realization: "It took three or four years before I realized that I could stay in a job, that this was more like no job at all. I had complete freedom . . . I could do what I wanted to do, and there were no comments. It was simply perfect. You couldn't mention a better job. It was really no job at all."[18]

From Whaling Village to Scientific Research Center

When McClintock arrived at Cold Spring Harbor in the early 1940s she found a charming, unpretentious, somewhat rundown former whaling village. Nestled in one of the many harbors of Long Island Sound, the town had been (and would continue to be) retrofitted as a center for scientific research. The name of the town's main thoroughfare, Bungtown Road, recalled its whaling history: Oil made from whale blubber had been enclosed in barrels stoppered with so-called bungs. After the discovery of petroleum in Pennsylvania in 1859, the need for whale oil declined. For a while the factories, dwellings, and warehouses that had supported the once-thriving industry lay empty. After the Civil War, however, wealthy visitors began to vacation in the area. Some realized that the town, with its proximity to the water and its rural charm, would be a good site for scientific research. In 1890 a summertime marine biology teaching lab opened there. In the early twentieth century the Carnegie Institution of Washington, whose aims included strengthening American scientific research and education, established a laboratory there. In 1921 that lab gave rise to the Department of Genetics, which became McClintock's scientific home.

The oldest laboratory structure in the United States still used for scientific purposes is found at Cold Spring Harbor. It dates back to 1893. McClintock's lab was on the top floor of a somewhat older building, which everyone called the Animal House. The cages and pens that once held experimental animals had been replaced by microscopes and the other equipment geneticists needed for their mid-twentieth-century research. When McClintock took possession of her lab in the early 1940s she had no way of knowing that in 1971 the newly renovated Animal House would be renamed in her honor.

To make her lab functional for her own purposes, McClintock pushed several desks together so that she had a single long surface on which to work. An adjacent small room served as storage for her dried ears of corn, each one carefully labeled to indicate how she had crossed, or mated, it. Her lab would also serve as the living room in which she entertained. At least one geneticist was invited there for "better coffee, fresh orange juice, oatmeal or eggs, toast or English muffins (or both), marmalade or honey (or both), conversation."[19]

As a corn geneticist at Cold Spring Harbor, McClintock had very big shoes to fill. George Harrison Shull (1874–1954), the botanist and geneticist who became known as the father of hybrid corn, came to Cold Spring Harbor in 1906. Working in his cornfield to the north and east of the lab's main building, Shull made the initial observations that led to the development of hybrid corn. A hybrid is the offspring of parents of different varieties. One corn variety, for example, may resist disease better than another, while a second may fare better in cold weather than the other. The hybrid seeds that result from crossing—or mating—the two different varieties can grow into corn plants with *both* desirable traits. Shull's early work ultimately led to an increase in the yield of corn by 25 to 50 percent per acre.

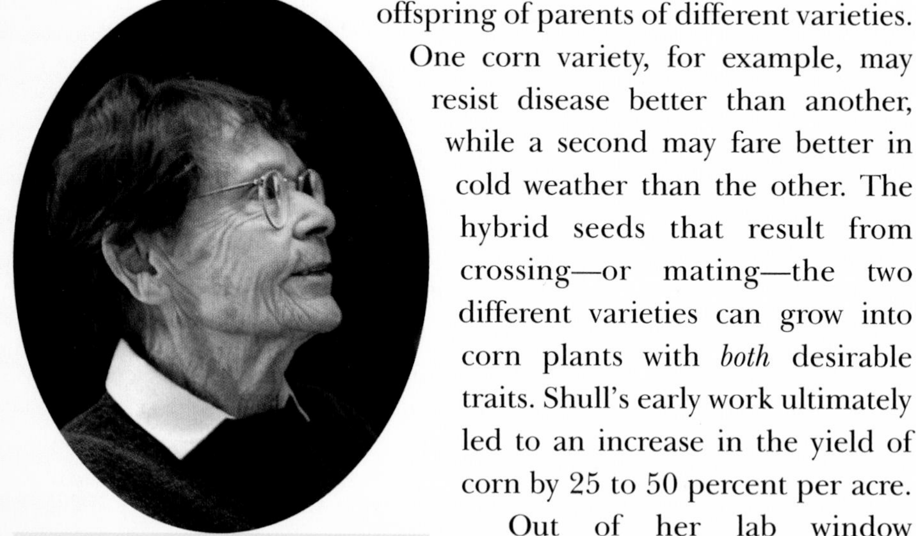

Barbara McClintock found both a personal and professional home upon her arrival at Cold Spring Harbor in the early 1940s.

Out of her lab window McClintock could look out on her own corn plot. It was large enough to hold many hundreds of plants. For research purposes she wanted diverse varieties of corn, so some of the plants were short, some bushy, some tall; some had large ears, while some had small ears. Other scientists played softball on a field near her corn plot, and the ball often ended up in the midst of her plants.

Softball was not the only leisure-time activity available to the scientific staff and visitors at Cold Spring Harbor. McClintock was able to indulge her passion for tennis. In addition she often took walks along the sea wall or in the wooded areas. Sometimes the purpose of her walks was to collect wild black walnuts for the brownies she enjoyed baking. Other times she focused on the natural world around her, often with a field guide in hand. She might have been a corn geneticist, but the amazing variety in nature in its entirety never failed to amaze her and fill her with awe.

Cold Spring Harbor Becomes McClintock's Home

CIW's Genetics Department at Cold Spring Harbor was more than McClintock's scientific home. For many years she lived in a dilapidated home across the highway from the entrance to the Department of Genetics. As she grew older and Route 25A grew busier, it became increasingly dangerous for her to cross the highway after dark. In the last few years of her life she lived on the campus, in a simple ground-floor apartment of Hooper House, a women's dormitory. She spent less time in either home, however, than in the lab, where she could be found nearly all day, seven days a week. Since she spent so little time at home, for over 40 years she had no phone there. Most meals she took in Blackford Hall, the lab's dining hall. Her diet was very simple, and when she ate at home, it consisted mostly of raw vegetables and easily prepared foods.

Summers were the busiest season at Cold Spring Harbor. Scientific visitors flocked there to take courses on a variety of topics. In addition, a summer symposium on a "hot" topic in biology had been held at the lab since 1933. These symposia attracted top scientists from around the world. The symposia were suspended following the entry of the United States into World War II in December 1941. They did not resume until 1946, after the war had ended.

The first postwar symposium was devoted to bacterial genetics. By the time McClintock arrived at Cold Spring Harbor in the early 1940s, some of the scientific visitors were already deeply involved in the study of bacteriophage—ß, a virus that attacks bacteria. Soon the lab would become a world-class center for microbiology, the study of microscopic organisms like bacteria, molds, viruses, and yeast, and for molecular biology, the study of the molecules that direct molecular processes in cells. Genetic information, for example, is stored in large molecules in an organism's cells. Molecular biologists study the way these molecules change that genetic information into chemical reactions that result in an organism's traits.

One aim of the microbiologists was to discover the physical laws that underlie all of genetics by studying simple, tiny life forms. By the late 1940s Cold Spring Harbor had become, as one of its directors later wrote, "*the* site to which the best and the brightest of the gene-dominated scientific world came to meet for the exchange of ideas."[20] While most of the scientists at Cold Spring Harbor were hoping to advance the study of genetics by studying tiny bacteria and viruses, McClintock continued to grow a yearly crop of corn to study individual kernels under a regular microscope. To many, her work no longer seemed on the cutting edge.

McClintock recognized within a few years of her arrival that she had found a good home with CIW at Cold Spring Harbor. Like many people, however, she found that even home seemed unwelcoming sometimes. Periodically she expressed deep dissatisfaction with her environment. For example, in May 1945 she wrote her old friend George Beadle, now at Stanford University, "It is so dull and uninspired here . . . . I am a little afraid to remain here."[21] During the half-century she lived and worked as a CIW geneticist at Cold Spring Harbor, she did some important work elsewhere. For example, in the winter of 1944 Beadle himself asked for her help in working out the cytology of the pink bread mold he was studying. During the ten weeks she spent with him at Stanford, she established the number of chromosomes of this mold and showed how they move during cell division. Her work enabled Beadle to proceed with the research that earned him a Nobel Prize in 1958. As Beadle's biographers have noted, for McClintock this successful bit of research was "only a minor triumph in her illustrious career."[22] For another scientist it might have been the achievement of a lifetime.

Sometimes professional trips away from Cold Spring Harbor were enough to restore McClintock's enthusiasm for her own primary work with her beloved corn. Sometimes, however, the mere thought of packing for a trip left her longing to get back to the informal life on campus. For example, in late 1949 the president of the Carnegie Institution of Washington asked her to present a lecture to the trustees. In a letter to her good friend and colleague Marcus Rhoades she looked forward to returning home even before she left. The packing, she found, was "a chore with the addition of a great clothes burden for decorating the body . . . requiring taking three suits and a dinner dress with all that goes with it—and that ain't little! Can't wait to get back!"[23] Cold Spring Harbor might not have been perfect, but for better or for worse it was the only real home she had for the rest of her life.

7

"Jumping Genes" and "Controlling Elements"

ONE OF THE THINGS MCCLINTOCK LOVED about her position at CIW's Department of Genetics at Cold Spring Harbor was that she could devote herself to whatever work she wished. She had no teaching responsibilities, and her paycheck came regularly, whatever work she pursued. She chose to continue studying the breakage–fusion–bridge cycle she had discovered at the University of Missouri. Having developed a way to use the cycle itself to produce mutations in her corn, she could advance her genetic investigations without the need for expensive and dangerous X-ray equipment.

The year 1944 was a momentous one for McClintock in more ways than one. The significance of her election that year to the National Academy of Sciences hit her right away. As only the third woman to be elected in the academy's eighty-one-year history, she wrote a friend, "I must admit I was stunned. Jews, women and Negroes are accustomed to discrimination and don't expect much. I am not a feminist, but I am always gratified when illogical barriers are broken—for Jews, women, Negroes, etc. It helps all of us."[1]

The significance of her work that year would not become apparent for some time. In her Nobel lecture, however, she said, "The experiment that alerted me to the mobility of specific components of genomes . . . commenced with the growing of approximately 450 plants in the summer of 1944." Within a few years her study of patterns of color and colorlessness on the kernels of these plants led her to the discovery of "transposable elements that could regulate gene expression in precise ways. Because of this I called them 'controlling elements.' Their origins and their actions were a focus of my research for many years thereafter."[2]

A younger woman geneticist who came to Cold Spring Harbor in the summer of 1944 later remembered that "the greatest thrill was the opportunity to follow closely Barbara McClintock's discovery of transposable elements and her elucidation of their role in controlling gene expression. I was able to look over her shoulder often as her careful experiments began to tell her what the patterns of spots on her maize kernels meant."[3]

By the spring of 1948 McClintock had identified two genetic elements that could change positions on the chromosome. She shared with her younger colleague her conviction that these were not genes, strictly speaking. Instead these mobile genetic elements acted like switches that could activate or deactivate specific

Barbara McClintock at work in her lab at Cold Spring Harbor on March 26, 1947.

genes. For example, the movement of a genetic element into a gene responsible for purple pigment could switch that gene off, resulting in a colorless kernel. But if the segment later moved out of that gene in some cells, the switch in those cells would be reactivated, yielding kernels with purple spots. Following McClintock's work on a daily basis, the younger scientist came to believe that, like her older colleague, she could "actually see genes turning on and off."[4] McClintock believed that the controlling elements could explain how so many different types of cells and tissues could develop in the same organism, even though every cell in the organism had an identical set of genes. It all depended on which genes were switched on and which were switched off during the organism's development.

By the spring of 1948 geneticist Salvador Luria had learned about McClintock's discovery of transposition and her developing theory. Since he had been studying bacteriophage at Cold Spring Harbor for some summers by then, Luria knew McClintock. Even though his specialty was bacteriophage genetics, he thought the work of this eminent maize geneticist was important enough that he presented it in a seminar to the geneticists at his home institution, the University of Indiana.[5]

Dismay and Despair After Going Public

Whether or not she knew of Luria's interest in her work, McClintock was hesitant to publish her results. In early 1950 she told her old friend and colleague Charlie Burnham, "You can see why I have not dared publish an account of this story. There is so much that is completely new and the implications are so suggestive of an altered concept of gene mutation that I have not wanted to make any statements until the evidence was conclusive enough to make me confident of the validity of the concepts."[6] Before she went public, she had to be fully confident that what she was proposing was validated by what she saw. After all, her theory was completely at odds with the general belief that genetic material remained unchanged as it passed from one generation to the next.

By the time of the Cold Spring Harbor Summer Symposium of 1951, McClintock clearly felt confident enough to present her work in a long, complicated presentation to the three hundred scientists in attendance. Note that she, who had been working with corn for more than two decades and painstakingly carrying out experiments with broken chromosomes for nearly as long, had nonetheless required several years to convince herself of the validity of her conclusions. What happened over the next few years may show that she simply expected too much, too quickly, of colleagues who lacked her particular research interests and background. On some level she seems to have understood this. In unpublished notes she wrote as she worked on her Nobel acceptance speech in 1983, she wrote: "At first I was surprised that the phenomenon [of controlling elements] was so unacceptable. . . . If [others] had had the same fantastic experiences with the maize plant as I was having, they would have drawn the same conclusion. The evidence and logic were incontestable."[7] The point, of course, is that no one but McClintock herself had those experiences.

By the time she made her presentation, other corn geneticists had confirmed the fact that transposition occurs in maize. The genetics community seemed prepared to accept this phenomenon as true, at least for corn. Although there were no questions following the presentation, pictures taken at the symposium show McClintock engaged in lively conversation with her fellow scientists. An article summarizing the meeting in the journal *Science* mentions that her paper "aroused particular interest."[8] Geneticist Salvador Luria later recalled his impression of her presentation: "There was Barbara McClintock, a tiny but formidable scientist, speaking as fast as anyone I knew and packing years of work into a one-hour lecture. Her discoveries in maize genetics had to wait decades before being appreciated as opening new paths in biology."[9] In any case, McClintock's letters to colleagues that summer show no indication that she felt snubbed. Yet McClintock would later claim that she was shocked by the total lack of interest in her talk and that she felt shunned by the scientific community in its aftermath.

Following that summer's symposium, McClintock published only one article on controlling elements in a major scientific journal. That article came out in 1953. McClintock later recalled receiving "only three requests" for copies of that paper. The lack of enthusiasm for her work led her to conclude "that no amount of published evidence would be effective" in convincing others of the significance of her discovery.[10]

As it happened, in1953, the genetics community and the public at large were completely absorbed in another exciting scientific development in the world of genetics. James Watson, who would later become the director of Cold Spring Harbor Laboratory, and his colleague Francis Crick had recently figured out and described the molecular structure of DNA. That extremely long molecule transfers genetic characteristics in all life forms. Whatever attention the popular press was prepared to devote to scientific work was reserved for this discovery. Scientists, too, were perhaps too caught up in this triumph of molecular biology to pay very much attention to McClintock's work.

For whatever reason, McClintock now fell into the depths of despair. She was particularly upset when "friends" confided in her that a well-known geneticist had called her "just an old bag who'd been hanging around CSH for years."[11] In a letter to her old friend Beadle she complained that "the environment [at Cold Spring Harbor] is so limited both intellectually and spiritually" that "it may not be possible for me to remain here."[12] The following month she sent a letter of resignation to Vannevar Bush, the president of the Carnegie Institution of Washington, even though she had no idea of where she might seek a better position.[13]

Beadle reminded her that she had done such wonderful work two decades earlier when she had been a National Research Council Fellow, with access to the facilities at several different institutions. He advised her to ask CIW's President Bush for a similar appointment. If the Carnegie would guarantee her salary, Beadle could offer her free access to his own facilities at Stanford. Marcus Rhoades, their colleague, was also ready to welcome her at the University of Illinois (where he had gone after leaving Columbia University).

In order to keep McClintock from resigning, the Carnegie Institution accepted this novel suggestion. Perhaps the mere indication that she was valued enough to be granted such an unconventional position convinced her to remain at Cold Spring Harbor. Still, she never relinquished the belief, whether valid or not, that she had been shunned by an unwelcoming genetics community that failed immediately to recognize the importance of her work.

Keeping Professionally Active

One myth about McClintock is that her feeling of rejection led her to hide herself away from the larger community of scientists. That story is only partly true. She continued to work by herself, following her interests where they took her. While most of her research records ended up in file cabinets in her office, she did write up annual summaries of her work to be published in the Carnegie Institution Year Books. In 1973 she wrote a British geneticist, "I stopped publishing detailed reports long ago when I realized, and acutely, the extent of disinterest and lack of confidence in the conclusions I was drawing from the studies . . . . I decided it was useless to add weight to the biologist's wastebasket. Instead, I decided to use the added time to enlarge experiments and thus increase my comprehensions of the basic phenomena."[14]

She did not hide in her office, however. She accepted invitations to lecture about her work at numerous institutions, including, among others, Caltech, Brandeis University, Columbia University, and Cornell.[15] Beginning in 1957, she participated in a maize research project in Latin America. Funded by the National Science Foundation and the Rockefeller Foundation, she helped trace the origins of races of maize in that part of the world. Together with two young scientists whom she trained, she published the results of this work in 1981. The book, *The Chromosomal Constitution of Races of Maize*, has influenced several fields, including ethnobotany (the study of the plant lore and agricultural customs of different cultures), paleobotany (the study of fossil plants), and evolutionary botany (the study of how plants change over time)[16] She also made it her business to keep up her knowledge of new developments in genetics, microbiology, and molecular biology. If people were less interested (at least in her view) in what she was doing, she would remain interested in what they were doing. In the late 1970s, she told her first biographer, "I was being educated, and it was an opportunity for me I do not regret; in fact, I think it was a great opportunity not to be listened to, but to listen."[17]

In the meantime she had the pleasure of seeing her work written up in textbooks and referred to in journals. As early as 1959 her first paper about jumping genes, published the year before her Cold Spring Harbor Symposium, was included, along with her 1931 crossing-over paper, in a book called *Classic Papers in Genetics.*[18]

Keeping up to date with the research breakthroughs in the field paid off the following year. In 1960 two French microchemists, one of whom she had known since the 1930s, when they overlapped at Caltech, explained how genes were regulated in bacteria. When they failed to acknowledge her work, she wrote an article herself that clarified the link between her controlling elements and their "operons." The article appeared in *The American Naturalist* in early 1961. In the symposium at Cold Spring Harbor that summer the two French scientists gave McClintock explicit credit in their concluding remarks: "Long before regulator genes and operators were recognized in bacteria, the extensive and penetrating work of McClintock . . . had revealed the existence, in maize, of two classes of genetic 'controlling elements' . . . ."[19] The French scientists, Jacques Monod and François Jacob, shared a Nobel prize in 1965 for their work.

Just as 1944 was a notable year for McClintock, so was 1967. In that year she was chosen by a committee of important geneticists for the National Academy of Sciences' Kimber Medal, the highest honor awarded specifically to a geneticist. Marcus Rhoades expressed his support for this award by writing, "One of the remarkable things about Barbara McClintock's surpassingly beautiful investigations is that they came solely from her own labors. Without technical help of any kind, she has by virtue of her boundless energy, her complete devotion to science, her originality and ingenuity, and her quick and high intelligence made a series of significant discoveries unparalleled in the history of cytogenetics."[20]

In June of 1967 McClintock turned sixty-five. At that time the Carnegie Institution required researchers to retire upon reaching that age. McClintock had no intention of stopping her research, however. In recognition of her extraordinary accomplishments to date and in anticipation of her continued contributions, the Carnegie Institution conferred a very great honor on her. McClintock was named a Distinguished Service Member. According to biochemist-geneticist Maxine Singer, a former president of the Carnegie Institution, as a Distinguished Service Member, McClintock's "research was still supported by Carnegie and Carnegie paid rent to Cold Spring Harbor for her laboratory until she died."[21]

As a younger scientist put it, "retirement" was in some ways the "most rewarding phase" in McClintock's career, "during which she would have the pleasure of watching the scientific world catch up with her."[22]

8 One of the Intellectual Giants of Her Time

FROM 1965 TO 1974 MCCLINTOCK SPENT A WEEK or two every spring semester at Cornell as an Andrew D. White Professor. She was one of a small number of distinguished individuals invited to participate in a program named for Cornell's first president. During her visit in 1970 she asked a nervous new assistant professor, "Do you think that there are transposable elements in yeast?" Years later he recalled how he "stuck to the prejudice of the time—I thought that transposable elements, or 'McClintock elements,' were something special to corn, so I never even thought about such things in yeast."[1] The young professor's attitude was indeed symptomatic of the time. Scientists who knew of McClintock's work tended to think it was something peculiar to maize.

"The Prejudice of the Time"

McClintock was very aware of this "prejudice of the time." The sense of being unappreciated by her colleagues was very painful to her. By 1973, however, a British geneticist was able to write her, "I think you are too despondent about the impact which your work has had. It's true that it took a long time for the implications to begin to sink in. This wasn't, I think, due to lack of clarity in what you said and wrote—it was rather that people couldn't see how on earth it all related to anything else that they knew about. Something that can't be fitted into any existing framework of knowledge and ideas tends to get pushed out of mind, even if it isn't actually disbelieved. I think that genetics has now very nearly caught up and geneticists are now likely to be very much more receptive to what you have been reporting all these years."[2]

Confirmation From Molecular Biology

As one Nobel laureate geneticist later commented, it was the work of molecular biologists over the 1970s and 1980s that helped scientists "integrate the startling evidence she presented into a coherent scheme."[3] Once molecular biologists discovered transposition in bacteria, viruses, and—despite the young Cornell professor's reservations—yeast, scientists began to see how important mobile genetic elements were. Soon it became apparent that they played a major role in public health. An article on "Transposable Genetic Elements" in *Scientific American* in early 1980 explained the connection between transposition and the spread of antibiotic resistance. It also confirmed McClintock's assertion that "transposable genetic elements can serve as biological switches, turning genes on or off as a consequence of their insertion at specific locations."[4] One of the authors of that article later said, "Transposable elements are an example of how new ideas are accepted coldly by the scientific community . . . first they said she's crazy; then they said it's peculiar to maize; then they said it's everywhere but has no significance; and then finally they woke up to its significance."[5]

Many of the discoveries supporting McClintock's work were made by molecular biologists associated with Cold Spring Harbor. In the summer of 1980 the Cold Spring Harbor Symposium was devoted to the topic of "Movable Genetic Elements." Among the many topics discussed were the relationship between transposons (as they were often called) and cancer, and the use of artificial transposons to carry genes from one species to another as a way of producing chemicals for medical use. In 1989 Nina Fedoroff, a young geneticist, gave a special evening lecture at the Washington, DC, headquarters of the Carnegie Institution of Washington. Fedoroff described how she and her colleagues had succeeded over the past decade in doing the molecular biology necessary to extract transposons from maize. McClintock was the guest of honor that evening.[6]

Attaining and Using Public Fame

The public at large also became increasingly more aware of McClintock and her work during the 1970s and 1980s. In May 1971 McClintock was among the scientists upon whom President Richard Nixon bestowed the National Medal of Science. The president's remarks to those being honored doubtless made scientists and science educators everywhere grit their teeth: "I have read [explanations of your scientific work] and I want you to know that I do not understand them. But I want you to know, too, that because I do not understand them, I realize how enormously important their contributions are to this Nation. That, to me, is the nature of science to the unsophisticated people."[7]

Two years later Ernst Caspari, a friend and colleague, wrote McClintock, "You are . . . very famous now, and it is rather astonishing how your fame has increased at a time of life where in most people it is on the way down."[8] McClintock's spreading fame during the decade of the 1970s is reflected in the number of honorary degrees she collected from prestigious institutions, including Williams College, Brandeis University, Harvard University, and Rockefeller University.

McClintock had not yet reached the peak of her fame, however. As shunned as she had felt in the 1950s and 1960s, in 1981 she began to feel overwhelmed by the media attention focused on her as she won several major awards. In October she won a $50,000 prize in medicine from the Wolf Foundation. Her old friend George Beadle had recently been diagnosed with cancer when he learned of the award. Nonetheless, he took pen to paper to express his pleasure. Even though "Beets" admitted having been "skeptical" in "the early stages of your most remarkable work," he told "Barb" that her work "should have been recognized long ago."[9]

In early November, Marcus Rhoades, another old friend, had been asked to evaluate McClintock's nomination for a so-called "genius award"—a grant from the MacArthur Foundation. Rhoades wrote, "Barbara McClintock is one of the intellectual giants of her time."[10] In the middle of the month the foundation announced their selection of McClintock as the first MacArthur Laureate, with a stipend of $60,000 a year, tax-free, for the rest of her life. The following day she received a $15,000 prize, the Albert Lasker Basic Medical Research Award.

Money and what it can buy were never very important to McClintock. She told a *New York Times* reporter, "I never wanted to be bothered by possessions, or to own anything . . . . When I was much younger, I used to say I wanted two things—to own an automobile and eyeglasses. Now I just want my eyeglasses."[11] Still, she did use some of the money to buy a new car and to improve her living quarters.

When news of McClintock's Lasker prize spread, people noted that in the 35 years since the award had been established, nearly half of its recipients had gone on to win the Nobel Prize. Nonetheless, she was taken by surprise in October 1983, when she heard on the radio (she still had no telephone at home) that she had become the seventh woman ever to win a Nobel. Only two women scientists before her (Marie Curie in 1911 and Dorothy Hodgkin in 1964) had been awarded unshared prizes.

According to a newspaper account, "When Barbara McClintock learned she had won the Nobel Prize in Medicine, she was heard to exclaim, 'Oh, dear,' and then she walked out into the brisk morning air to pick walnuts. She is like that. She is known for baking with black walnuts . . . . The 81-year-old Dr. McClintock, dressed in dungarees and carrying tongs for grappling the walnuts, left her apartment on the grounds of the Cold Spring Harbor Laboratory and strolled alone along a wooded path down by an inlet of the Long Island Sound . . . She must have been bracing herself for the applause. For when she returned from her walk, Dr. McClintock told . . . the laboratory's administrative director, 'I will do what I have to do.'"[12]

What she had to do was hold a press conference. She told the reporters assembled in the auditorium at Cold Spring Harbor that she had no idea how much money was associated with the prize. When told it was approximately $190,000, McClintock said, "I'll just have to get to one side and think about this." When asked why it had taken so long for the importance of her work to be recognized, she answered, "Oh, it was quite all right. It took long, I think, because nobody had the experience I had."[13] She acknowledged her gratitude to the institution that had been paying her salary for over forty years: "I don't think there could be

Barbara McClintock's work studying maize continues to have an impact on our daily lives today.

a finer institution for allowing you to do what you want to do. Now, if I had been at some other place, I'm sure that I would have been fired for what I was doing, because nobody was accepting it, but the Carnegie Institution never once told me that I shouldn't be doing it. They never once said I should publish when I wasn't publishing."[14]

Nobel laureates often use the fame that is thrust upon them as a platform to promote issues they care about deeply. Although less vociferously than others, McClintock did so as well. While she never thought of herself as a feminist, she had suffered enough snubs as a woman scientist to want to help improve the lot of younger women in the field. For example, she had been "deeply offended" in the 1970s by the male president of the Carnegie Institution of Washington. As the husband of a professor of pediatrics at a major university, he should have known better than to ask McClintock— "already a distinguished scientist, long a member of the National Academy of Sciences"— to make a special trip to Washington to "chat with the wives of the members of the board of trustees during the annual meeting."[15] She was also offended—though amused at the same time— when an invitation to a dinner for Nobel laureates came from Henry Kissinger, the former Secretary of State, who was at the time head of a national commission on Central America. The names of all the male guests were listed on the invitation preceded by the title "Dr." McClintock, who had earned her doctorate over a half century earlier, was listed as "Ms. B. McClintock." She sent the offending invitation to her younger colleague, Dr. Evelyn Witkin (the Barbara McClintock Professor of Genetics at Rutgers University), with the following words handwritten in the margin: "I don't get no respect!"[16]

Though she could laugh at times at the snubs she herself experienced, she understood that discrimination against women in the scientific workplace was no laughing matter. As a result, on January 14, 1991, McClintock wrote a letter to the president of the National Academy of Sciences, urging him "to initiate a bold new start" to "increase the participation of women scientists" in the activities both of the NAS itself and of its National Research Council, which provides a variety of services to the government, the public, and the scientific and engineering communities.[17]

The McClintock Legacy

That same year preparations began to create a special gift to celebrate McClintock's forthcoming ninetieth birthday in June 1992. When Nina Fedoroff lectured at Cold Spring Harbor in 1991 on the molecular genetics of the maize transposable elements, a representative of the Cold Spring Harbor Press approached her. He suggested publishing a volume of essays, to be written by scientists whose careers had meshed with McClintock's one way or another over the years. Fedoroff overcame her "qualms that Barbara would find this not a gift but another burden," and together with her colleague David Botstein collected "varied essays each reflecting the pursuits and passions ignited by the sparks and embers scattered from the fierce blaze of McClintock's intellect through the decades of this century of genetics."[18]

Many of the authors of the book that resulted, *The Dynamic Genome: Barbara McClintock's Ideas in the Century of Genetics*, were among those attending a quiet ninetieth birthday party on the porch of the home of Jim Watson, then director of Cold Spring Harbor Laboratory. McClintock was completely surprised by the gift of the volume. As Fedoroff recalled, "soon her face began to glow as she perceived the depth of understanding and respect gathered around her, lovingly collected between the covers of the book. She said later it was the best party ever for her, though she admitted that it had taken a week to recover at her age."[19]

In fact, her age had barely slowed McClintock down. Although both her eyesight and her hearing had recently deteriorated, through her eighties she continued to put in long days at her office. Nonetheless, she had begun to tell people that she expected to make it to ninety—the maximum age people in her family seemed to reach—but not much beyond.

On Thursday, July 30, 1992, the subject of McClintock's ninetieth birthday was brought up in an unlikely setting. McClintock's congressman, the Honorable Gary L. Ackerman, the Democrat representing District Five of New York, rose in the House of Representatives "to honor a distinguished pioneer of genetic biology, Dr. Barbara McClintock," who had recently celebrated both her ninetieth birthday and the completion of a half-century of research at Cold Spring Harbor.[20] A little more than a month later McClintock died in a Long Island hospital, after a brief illness.

In the years following McClintock's death, several

biographies of McClintock were published, and numerous researchers in a variety of fields traced their work back to hers. In a review of a 2001 biography of her mentor, Nina Fedoroff summarized McClintock's achievement: "We know that transposons are astonishingly abundant, comprising a majority of the DNA in some species. We know that transposon-like rearrangements are essential to our immune system and that transposons maintain telomeres, at least in certain kinds of fly. And, we know that transposons are at the heart of genomic restructuring on an evolutionary time scale . . . . She might not have got everything right, but she sure got a lot of it—a track record to die for."[21]

In that review Fedoroff also expressed her own belief that McClintock's decision to remain single may have contributed to her professional success: "And I, for one, am profoundly grateful that she focused all of her formidable intellect on science and did not divide it among picking up the children, cooking dinner, listening to her husband's ideas, shopping, cleaning—and doing genetics."[22]

In a private letter Fedoroff clarified what she did not mean to imply in that comment: "It was NOT the idea that one has to stay single to succeed!" Rather, Fedoroff believed that a combination of self-knowledge and good fortune contributed to McClintock's extraordinary success. Her self-knowledge kept her free of the chores of both married and academic life. Her good fortune in being supported by the Carnegie

Institution of Washington "allowed McClintock the freedom to discover, to see what others would not see for another 30 years."

Fedoroff also pointed out that McClintock's personality might have made it hard for her to succeed as a scientist in the twenty-first century. Scientists today spend much of their time applying for grants to support their research. Working on the budgets and other details of grant proposals constitutes just the kind of busy work that McClintock detested and that drove her out of academic life. According to Fedoroff, "Barbara often said that she could not have become a scientist in the present world of grants—it would have driven her to do something else."[23]

We will never know whether Barbara McClintock would have found a way to do her science in the second century of genetics. What is clear, however, is that in the twenty-first century the profound implications of McClintock's pioneering work continue to unfold, and the story of her life continues to intrigue and inspire.

Activities

Activity One: Using Punnett Squares

As a student, McClintock would have learned how to use a kind of genetic checkerboard called a Punnett square. The square is named for British geneticist Reginald Punnett (1875–1967), the author of an early genetics textbook. Punnett devised the square as a table for the visual display of genetic information. You can also learn to use Punnett squares to display the results of a cross between pea plants.

Today we know that genes determine the characteristics or traits of life forms. Plants and animals inherit a gene for each trait from each of their parents. The gene for a single trait, however, can come in different forms, known as alleles. The traits carried on some alleles are dominant, while the traits carried on other alleles are recessive. For example, the trait for tallness is dominant in pea plants.

The sum total of the alleles the organism inherits from its parents make up that organism's genotype. If an organism inherits identical alleles for a certain trait, one from each parent, the organism is said to be homozygous for that trait. By contrast, a heterozygous organism has two different alleles for a single trait, such as an allele for tallness and an allele for shortness.

The way an organism appears is called its phenotype. An organism's genotype determines its phenotype, but examining the phenotype alone does not reveal an organism's genotype. A recessive allele may be present in the organism's genotype but not visible to the eye in the phenotype. For example, a tall pea plant may have either two "tall" alleles or one "tall" allele and one "short" allele.

Before you can predict the genotype and phenotype of offspring, you must know the parents' genotypes. A Punnett square is a way of organizing information about the parents' genotypes in order to predict the likely genotypes and phenotypes of their offspring.

PART A

Make a Punnett square to predict the genotypes and phenotypes of the offspring produced by crossing a homozygous tall plant with a homozygous short plant. You need to designate which is the female and which is the male plant so that steps 1 and 2 are easy to follow. It might also be useful to provide abbreviations, like *T* for the dominant allele, and *t* for the recessive allele.

1. Write the possible alleles inherited from the female parent along the left side of the square.
2. Write the possible alleles inherited from the male parent across the top of the square.
3. In each of the four boxes inside the square,

write the outcome of the combination of the female allele and the male allele.

4. What can you conclude about the genotypes of the four offspring of the homozygous short female and the homozygous tall male? What can you conclude about their phenotypes?

PART B

1. Following the same steps, make a Punnett square to predict the genotypes and phenotypes of the offspring produced by crossing a heterozygous tall male with a heterozygous tall female. Remember that

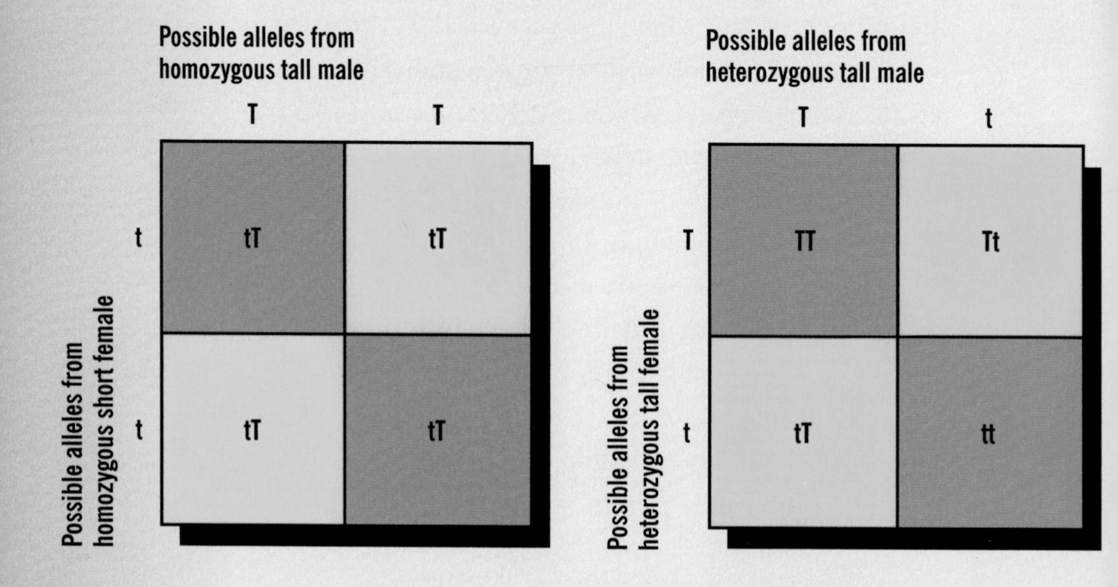

a heterozygous organism has both a dominant and a recessive allele.

2. How many offspring have the same genotype? How many have the same phenotype?
3. Among the offspring, what is the ratio of tall plants to short plants?

PART C

1. Following the same steps, make a Punnett square to predict the genotypes and phenotypes of the offspring produced by crossing a homozygous short pea plant and a heterozygous tall pea plant.
2. How do the offspring of this cross differ from the offspring in Part B?

▶ Activity Two: Your Own Dominant and Recessive Traits

Purpose:

To observe your phenotype and predict your genotype for each of two human traits

Materials needed:

- mirror
- hand lens

PART A

1. Holding the mirror in one hand, use your other hand to push your hair back. Notice whether there is a peak in the middle of your hairline or whether it falls in a straight line. A dominant allele, *W*, is responsible for the peaked hairline, known as a widow's peak. The straight hairline is a recessive allele, designated *w*.
2. In a data table like the one shown, record your phenotype for this trait in the top left square.
3. Record your possible genotypes for this trait in the top right square.

PART B

1. Using the hand lens, observe the middle finger on each of your hands to see whether it is covered with hair. A dominant allele, H, is responsible for hair on middle fingers. A recessive allele, h, is responsible for a hairless middle finger.
2. Record your phenotype for this trait in the bottom left square.
3. Record your possible genotypes for this trait.

Data Table

	Phenotype	Possible genotype
Hairline		
Middle digit of fingers		

Analysis and Conclusions

1. What dominant alleles do you know you have inherited? What recessive alleles?
2. Assuming you are unaware of your parents' phenotypes, can you be sure of any of your genotypes? Explain.

Chronology

1902—Born on June 16, in Hartford, Connecticut.

1908—Moves with family to Brooklyn, New York.

1923—Receives her B.S. from Cornell.

1927—Receives her Ph.D. from Cornell.

1927–31—Instructor in botany at Cornell (identifies the 10 corn chromosomes, discovers with Harriet Creighton the first proof that genetic crossing-over is accompanied by actual physical interchange of parts).

1931–33—National Research Council Fellow at the University of Missouri, Caltech, and Cornell.

1933–1934—Guggenheim Fellow in Germany.

1934–36—Researcher, Cornell, funded by the Rockefeller Foundation.

1936–42—Assistant Professor of Genetics, University of Missouri at Columbia.

1941-1942—Guest investigator, Department of Genetics, Carnegie Institution of Washington, at Cold Spring Harbor, New York, on leave of absence from the University of Missouri.

1942—Resigns from the University of Missouri.

1943–1967—Full-time researcher in genetics, the

Carnegie Institution of Washington (discovers genetic transposition and transposable elements, or "jumping genes").

1944—Elected to the National Academy of Sciences (Botany Section).

1945—Became first woman ever elected president of the Genetics Society of America.

1946—Elected to the American Philosophical Society.

1947—Awarded the American Association of University Women Achievement Award.

1951—Lectures at the Cold Spring Harbor Symposium on theories of "controlling elements" in maize.

1953—Almost resigns from the Carnegie Institution of Washington's Department of Genetics at Cold Spring Harbor.

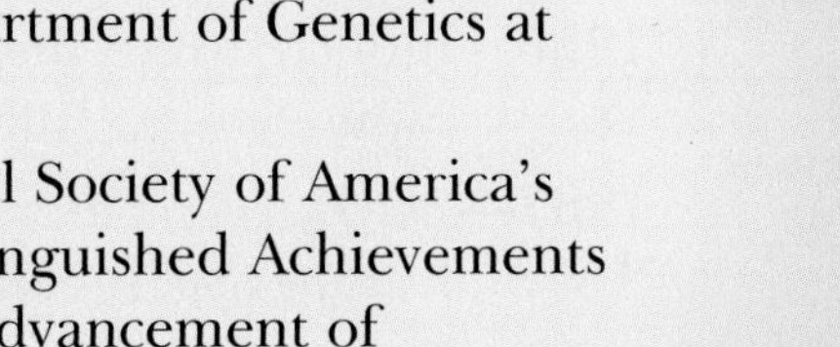

1957—Receives the Botanical Society of America's Merit Award for Distinguished Achievements in Contributions to Advancement of Botanical Sciences.

1957–81—Does research in South America on origins of maize.

1959—Elected to the American Academy of Arts and Sciences.

1965–74—Gives an annual series of lectures and works closely with graduate students as an Andrew D. White Professor at Cornell.

1967—Upon retirement becomes Distinguished Service Member of the Carnegie Institution of Washington.

1971—Receives the 1970 National Medal of Science from President Richard M. Nixon, becoming the first woman to be thus honored; the building housing McClintock's laboratory at Cold Spring Harbor is renamed the McClintock Laboratory.

1981—Receives the Wolf Prize; the first MacArthur Foundation Grant, a lifetime award; and the Albert and Mary Lasker Basic Medical Research Award; shares the Thomas Hunt Morgan Medal of the Genetics Society of America with Marcus M. Rhoades.

1983—Receives the Nobel Prize in Physiology or Medicine, becoming the third woman to win an unshared prize, and the first woman to win an unshared prize in Physiology or Medicine.

1986—Inducted into the National Women's Hall of Fame, Seneca Falls, New York.

1987—*The Discovery and Characterization of Transposable Elements: The Collected Papers of Barbara McClintock* is published.

1987–88—The Smithsonian National Museum of American History holds a special exhibit honoring McClintock.

1989—The Carnegie Institution of Washington establishes the Barbara McClintock Fellowship Fund.

1992—Receives *The Dynamic Genome: Barbara McClintock's Ideas in the Century of Genetics* at a ninetieth birthday party held at Cold Spring Harbor Laboratory; dies in Huntington, New York, on September 2.

1996—The DNA Learning Center at Cold Spring Harbor mounts "The World of Barbara McClintock," an exhibit exploring her research.

2001—Becomes the seventh scientist and first woman to be included in the National Library of Medicine's Profiles in Science website.

2005—The United States Postal Service issues a set of "American Scientists" postage stamps, honoring the work of McClintock and three male researchers, who helped shape twentieth-century science.

Chapter Notes

Chapter 1. The Original Big Mac

1. Mel Green, "Annals of Mobile DNA Elements in Drosophila: The Impact and Influence of Barbara McClintock," *The Dynamic Genome: Barbara McClintock's Ideas in the Century of Genetics*, eds. Nina Fedoroff and David Botstein (Plainview, New York: Cold Spring Harbor Laboratory Press, 1992), p. 122.

2. Nina V. Fedoroff and Nancy Marie Brown, *Mendel in the Kitchen: A Scientist's View of Genetically Modified Foods* (Washington, DC: Joseph Henry Press, 2004), p. 97.

Chapter 2. The Odd Member of the Family

1. Facts about McClintock's childhood come primarily from Evelyn Fox Keller, *A Feeling for the Organism: The Life and Work of Barbara McClintock* (San Francisco: W. H. Freeman and Company, 1983), pp. 17-36.

2. Evelyn Fox Keller, *A Feeling for the Organism: The Life and Work of Barbara McClintock* (San Francisco: W. H. Freeman and Company, 1983), p. 20.

3. Sharon Bertsch McGrayne, "Barbara McClintock," *Nobel Prize Women in Science: Their Lives, Struggles, and Momentous Discoveries*, 2nd ed. (Washington, DC: John Henry Press, 1998), p. 147.

4. Nathaniel C. Comfort, *The Tangled Field: Barbara McClintock's Search for the Patterns of Genetic Control* (Cambridge, MA: Harvard University Press, 2001), p. 20.

5. Evelyn Fox Keller, *A Feeling for the Organism: The Life and Work of Barbara McClintock* (San Francisco: W. H. Freeman, 1983), p. 75.

6. Ibid., p. 22.

7. Ibid., p. 23.

8. Ibid., p. 24.

9. McGrayne, "Barbara McClintock," p. 148.

10. Keller, p. 27.

11. Ibid., p. 26.

12. Ibid., p. 28.

13. Ibid., p. 26.

14. McGrayne, p. 149.

15. Keller, p. 30.

16. McGrayne, p. 149.

17. Keller, p. 31.

18. Keller, p. 30.

Chapter 3. The Three M's of Genetics

1. L. C. Dunn, *A Short History of Genetics: The Development of Some of the Main Lines of Thought: 1864-1939* (New York: McGraw-Hill Book Company, 1965), p. xiii.

2. Barbara McClintock, "The Significance of Responses of the Genome to Challenge," Nobel lecture, 8 December, 1983.

3. David Botstein, "Discovery of the Bacterial Transposon Tn10," *The Dynamic Genome: Barbara McClintock's Ideas in the Century of Genetics*, eds. Nina Fedoroff and David Botstein (Plainview, New York: Cold Spring Harbor Laboratory Press, 1992), p. 226.

4. J. A. Miller, "Nobel Prize to McClintock and Her Mobile Elements," *Science News*, vol. 124, Oct. 15, 1983, p. 244.

5. Nina V. Fedoroff and Nancy Marie Brown, *Mendel in the Kitchen: A Scientist's View of Genetically Modified Foods* (Washington, DC: Joseph Henry Press, 2004), p. 73.

6. Marcus M. Rhoades, "The Early Years of Maize Genetics," *The Dynamic Genome: Barbara McClintock's Ideas in the Century of Genetics*, eds. Nina Fedoroff and David Botstein (Plainview, New York: Cold Spring Harbor Laboratory Press, 1992), p. 45.

7. Sharon Bertsch McGrayne, "Barbara McClintock," *Nobel Prize Women in Science: Their Lives, Struggles, and Momentous Discoveries*, 2nd ed. (Washington, DC: Joseph Henry Press, 1998), p. 151.

8. James Watson, quoted in Helena Curtis and N. Sue Barnes, *Invitation to Biology*, 5th ed. (New York: Worth, 1994), p. 287.

Chapter 4. The Golden Age of Maize Cytogenetics at Cornell

1. Much of the material in this chapter is derived from the various papers of Lee B. Kass, as cited below.

2. Charlotte Williams Conable, *Women at Cornell: The Myth of Equal Education* (Ithaca and London: Cornell University Press, 1977), p. 8.

3. Ibid., pp. 142, 128.

4. Evelyn Fox Keller, *A Feeling for the Organism: The Life and Work of Barbara McClintock* (San Francisco: W. H. Freeman and Company, 1983), p. 31.

5. Lee B. Kass and William B. Provine, "Genetics in the roaring 20's: The influence of Cornell's professors and curriculum on Barbara McClintock's development as a cytogeneticist," *American Journal of Botany* , June 1997, vol. 84 (no. 6, Supplement), p. 123.

6. Nathaniel C. Comfort, *The Tangled Field: Barbara McClintock's Search for the Patterns of Genetic Control* (Cambridge, MA: Harvard University Press, 2001), p. 25.

7. Ira Herskowitz, "Controlling Elements, Mutable Alleles, and Mating-type Interconversion," in *The Dynamic Genome: Barbara McClintock's Ideas in the Century of Genetics,* eds. Nina Fedoroff and David Botstein (Plainview, New York: Cold Spring Harbor Laboratory Press, 1992), p. 295.

8. Helen V. Crouse, "Barbara McClintock: Recollections of a Graduate Student," in *The Dynamic Genome: Barbara McClintock's Ideas in the Century of Genetics,* eds. Nina Fedoroff and David Botstein (Plainview, New York: Cold Spring Harbor Laboratory Press, 1992), p. 28.

9. Evelyn Fox Keller, *A Feeling for the Organism: The Life and Work of Barbara McClintock* (San Francisco: W. H. Freeman, 1983), pp. 32–33.

10. Ibid., p. 34.

11. Sharon Bertsch McGrayne, "Barbara McClintock," *Nobel Prize Women in Science: Their Lives,*

Struggles, and Momentous Discoveries, 2nd ed. (Washington, DC: Joseph Henry Press, 1998), p. 154.

12. *Barbara McClintock, Autobiography*, <nobelprize.org/medicine/laureates/1983/mcclintock-autobio.html>

13. Ibid.

14. Lee B. Kass and William B. Provine, "Genetics in the roaring 20's: The influence of Cornell's professors and curriculum on Barbara McClintock's development as a cytogeneticist," *American Journal of Botany*, June 1997, vol. 84 (no. 6, Supplement), p. 123.

15. McClintock, *Autobiography*.

16. Lee B. Kass and William B. Provine, "Genetics in the roaring 20's: The influence of Cornell's professors and curriculum on Barbara McClintock's development as a cytogeneticist," *American Journal of Botany*, June 1997, vol. 84 (no. 6, Supplement), p. 123.

17. Lee B. Kass, "Records and Recollections: A New Look at Barbara McClintock, Nobel-Prize-Winning Geneticist," *Genetics*, Vol. 164 (August 2003), p. 1251. Also Lee B. Kass, "McClintock, Barbara," in Richard Robinson, editor, *Plant Sciences* (New York: Macmillan Reference USA, 2001), vol. 3, pp. 66-69.

18. Information about the Synapsis Club and the Razzberry Club comes from Paul Berg and Maxine Singer, *George Beadle, An Uncommon Farmer: The Emergence of Genetics in the 20th Century* (Cold Spring Harbor, NY: Cold Spring Harbor Laboratory Press, 2003), p. 45.

19. Paul Berg and Maxine Singer, *George Beadle, An Uncommon Farmer: The Emergence of Genetics in the 20th*

Century (Cold Spring Harbor, New York: Cold Spring Harbor Laboratory Press, 2003), p. 46.

20. L. B. Kass and R. P. Murphy, "Will the real Maize Genetics Garden please stand up?" *Maize Genetics Cooperation Newsletter*, vol. 77 (2003), pp. 41–43, (August 9, 2005). <http://www.maizegdb.org/mnl/77/79kass.html>

21. By poring through Emerson's correspondence in the Cornell University Archives, Lee B. Kass discovered why the relationship between McClintock and Randolph dissolved. Lee B. Kass, "Records and Recollections: A New Look at Barbara McClintock, Nobel-Prize-Winning Geneticist," *Genetics*, Vol. 164 (August 2003), p. 1251.

22. Marcus M. Rhoades, "The Early Years of Maize Genetics," *The Dynamic Genome: Barbara McClintock's Ideas in the Century of Genetics*, eds. Nina Fedoroff and David Botstein (Plainview, New York: Cold Spring Harbor Laboratory Press, 1992), p. 62.

23. Lee B. Kass, "Records and Recollections: A New Look at Barbara McClintock, Nobel-Prize-Winning Geneticist," *Genetics*, Vol. 164 (August 2003), p. 1251.

24. Lee B. Kass, "Records and Recollections: A New Look at Barbara McClintock, Nobel-Prize-Winning Geneticist," *Genetics* 164 (August 2003), p. 1254.

25. Lee B. Kass and Christophe Bonneuil, "Mapping and seeing: Barbara McClintock and the linking of genetics and cytology in maize genetics, 1928–35," in *Classical Genetic Research and Its Legacy: The Mapping Cultures of Twentieth-Century Genetics*, eds.

Hans-Jurg Rheinberger and Jean-Paul Gaudillière (Abingdon, UK: Routledge, 2004), p. 110.

26. McClintock, *Autobiography*.

27. Harriet B. Creighton, "Recollections of Barbara McClintock's Cornell Years," *The Dynamic Genome: Barbara McClintock's Ideas in the Century of Genetics*, eds. Nina Fedoroff and David Botstein (Plainview, New York: Cold Spring Harbor Laboratory Press, 1992), p. 16.

28. L. B. Kass and R. P. Murphy, "Will the real Maize Genetics Garden please stand up?" *Maize Genetics Cooperation Newsletter*, vol. 77 (2003), pp. 41–43.

29. Lee B. Kass, Christophe Bonneuil, and Edward H. Coe, Jr., "Cornfests, Cornfabs and Cooperation: The Origins and Beginnings of the Maize Genetics Cooperation News Letter," *Genetics* 169 (April 2005), p. 1787.

30. Rollins A. Emerson, letter to Lewis J. Stadler, January 14, 1930. In Kass and Bonneuil, p. 103.

31. McClintock, *Autobiography*.

32. Rhoades, "The Early Years of Maize Genetics," p. 63.

33. Creighton, "Recollections of Barbara McClintock's Cornell Years," p. 13.

34. Ibid., p. 14.

35. Edward Coe and Lee B. Kass, "Proof of physical exchange of genes on the chromosomes," *Proceedings of the National Academy of Sciences* (2005), vol. 102, no. 19, May 10, 2005, p. 6644.

36. Information about Creighton's role in the

crossing-over paper appears in Edward Coe and Lee B. Kass, "Proof of physical exchange of genes on the chromosomes," *Proceedings of the National Academy of Sciences* (2005), vol. 102, no. 19, May 10, 2005, pp. 6643, 6644.

37. James A. Peters, ed., *Classic Papers in Genetics* (Englewood Cliffs, NJ: Prentice-Hall, Inc., 1959), p. 156.

38. Berg and Singer, p. 48.

39. Nathaniel C. Comfort, *The Tangled Field: Barbara McClintock's Search for the Patterns of Genetic Control* (Cambridge, MA: Harvard University Press, 2001), p. 54.

40. "Endowed Professorships," *Cornell Chronicle*, vol. 35, no. 22, February 12, 2004, <www.news.cornell.edu/Chronicle/04/2.12.04/endowed_profs.html> (November 22, 2005).

Chapter 5. Fellowship at Home and Abroad

1. Information on the granting of fellowships to women scientists in the 1930s appears in Margaret W. Rossiter, *Women Scientists in America: Struggles and Strategies to 1940* (Baltimore: The Johns Hopkins University Press, 1982), pp. 269–272.

2. E-mail correspondence to the author from Lee B. Kass, 8/8/05, in the author's files.

3. Nathaniel C. Comfort, *The Tangled Field: Barbara McClintock's Search for the Patterns of Genetic Control* (Cambridge, MA: Harvard University Press, 2001), pp. 101–102.

4. Marcus M. Rhoades, "The Early Years of Maize Genetics," *The Dynamic Genome: Barbara McClintock's*

Ideas in the Century of Genetics, eds. Nina Fedoroff and David Botstein (Plainview, NY: Cold Spring Harbor Laboratory Press, 1992), p. 56.

5. Lee B. Kass and Christophe Bonneuil, "Mapping and seeing: Barbara McClintock and the linking of genetics and cytology in maize genetics, 1928–35," in *Classical Genetic Research and Its Legacy: The Mapping Cultures of Twentieth-Century Genetics*, eds. Hans-Jurg Rheinberger and Jean-Paul Gaudillière (Abingdon, UK: Routledge, 2004), p. 103.

6. Barbara McClintock, "The Significance of Responses of the Genome to Challenge," *Nobel Lecture*, 8 December, 1983, p. 183.

7. Quotations from the diary entry of Warren Weaver, April 17, 1934, quoted in Paul Berg and Maxine Singer, *George Beadle, An Uncommon Farmer: The Emergence of Genetics in the 20th Century* (Cold Spring Harbor, NY: Cold Spring Harbor Laboratory Press, 2003), p. 87.

8. Information about McClintock's memories of having lunch at the Athenaeum appears in Paul Berg and Maxine Singer, *George Beadle, An Uncommon Farmer: The Emergence of Genetics in the 20th Century* (Cold Spring Harbor, NY: Cold Spring Harbor Laboratory Press, 2003), p. 85.

9. Barbara McClintock, letter to Curt Stern, August 12, 1933 <http://profiles.nlm.nih.gov/LL/B/B/</D/_/llbmd.pdf> (August 9, 2005).

10. Paul Berg and Maxine Singer, p. 86.

11. Winifred Veronda, "James Bonner Recalls

Nobel Laureate Barbara McClintock, Caltech's First Woman Postdoc," *Caltech News*, February 1984, p. 3.

12. Margaret W. Rossiter, *Women Scientists in America: Struggles and Strategies to 1940* (Baltimore: The Johns Hopkins University Press, 1982), pp. 272–273.

13. Nathaniel C. Comfort, *The Tangled Field: Barbara McClintock's Search for the Patterns of Genetic Control* (Cambridge, MA: Harvard University Press, 2001), p. 60.

14. Evelyn Fox Keller. *A Feeling for the Organism: The Life and Work of Barbara McClintock* (San Francisco: W. H. Freeman and Company, 1983), p. 59.

15. Barbara McClintock, letter to Curt Stern, March 13, 1933 <http://profiles.nlm.nih.gov/LL/B/B/M/B/_/llbmb.pdf> (August 9, 2005).

16. Barbara McClintock, letter to Evelyn and Curt Stern, December 11, 1934 <http://profiles.nlm.nih.gov/LL/B/B/M/K/_/llbbmk.pdf> (August 9, 2005).

17. Barbara McClintock, letter to Evelyn and Curt Stern, March 4, 1934 <http://profiles.nlm.nih.gov/LL/B/B/M/J/_/llbbmj.pdf> (August 9, 2005).

18. Lee B. Kass and Christophe Bonneuil, "Mapping and seeing: Barbara McClintock and the linking of genetics and cytology in maize genetics, 1928–35," in *Classical Genetic Research and Its Legacy: The Mapping Cultures of Twentieth-Century Genetics*, eds., Hans-Jurg Rheinberger and Jean-Paul Gaudillière (Abingdon, UK: Routledge, 2004), p. 99.

19. Lee B. Kass, "Records and Recollections: A New Look at Barbara McClintock, Nobel-Prize-

Winning Geneticist," in *Genetics*, August 2003, vol. 164, p. 1251.

20. Lee B. Kass, "McClintock, Barbara," in Richard Robinson, editor, *Plant Sciences* (New York: Macmillan Reference USA, 2001), vol. 3, p. 68.

21. Warren Weaver, diary entry for June 24, 1934, quoted in Keller, pp. 73–74.

22. Barbara McClintock, letter to Charles Burnham, April 2, 1935 <http://profiles.nlm.nih.gov/LL/B/B/N/S/_/llbbns.pdf> (August 9, 2005).

23. Frank Blair Hanson, diary entry, August 1935, quoted in Keller, p. 75.

Chapter 6. From the Wrong Job to the Right One

1. L. B. Kass, "Missouri Compromise: tenure or freedom? New evidence clarifies why Barbara McClintock left academe," *Maize Genetics Cooperation Newsletter*, 2005 <http://www.agron.missouri.edu/mnl/79/05kass.htm> (August 9, 2005).

2. "The Barbara McClintock Papers, Breakage-Fusion-Bridge: The University of Missouri, 1936–1941" <http://profiles.nlm.nih.giv/LL/Views/Exhibit/narrative/missouri.html> (August 9, 2005).

3. Elof Axel Carlson, *Mendel's Legacy: The Origin of Classical Genetics* (Cold Spring Harbor, NY: Cold Spring Harbor Laboratory Press, 2004), pp. xviii, 240, 286.

4. Barbara McClintock, letter to Charles Burnham, August 9, 1940 <http://profiles.nlm.nih.gov/LL/Views/Exhibit/narrative/missouri.html> (August 9, 2005).

5. Barbara McClintock, letter to Charles Burnham, October 9, 1940 <http://profiles.nlm.nih.gov/LL/B/B/N/V/_/llbbnv.pdf> (August 9, 2005).

6. Barbara McClintock, letter to Charles Burnham, September 16, 1940 <http://profiles.nlm.nih.gov/LL/B/B/N/T/_/llbbnt.pdf> (August 9, 2005).

7. Barbara McClintock, letter to Charles Burnham, October 9, 1940 <http://profiles.nlm.nih.gov/LL/B/B/N/V/_/llbbnv.pdf> (August 9, 2005).

8. The discussion of McClintock's decision to leave the University of Missouri is based on L. B. Kass, "Missouri compromise: tenure or freedom? New evidence clarifies why Barbara McClintock left academe," *Maize Genetics Cooperation Newsletter* (2005) <http://www.agron.missouri.edu/mnl/79/05kass.htm> (August 9, 2005). See also Lee B. Kass, "Records and Recollections: A New Look at Barbara McClintock, Nobel-Prize-Winning Geneticist," *Genetics* 164, August 2003, pp. 1251–1260.

9. Lee B. Kass, "Records and Recollections: A New Look at Barbara McClintock, Nobel-Prize-Winning Geneticist," *Genetics* 164, August 2003, p. 1256.

10. Helen V. Crouse, "Barbara McClintock: Recollections of a Graduate Student," *The Dynamic Genome: Barbara McClintock's Ideas in the Century of Genetics*, eds. Nina Fedoroff and David Botstein (Plainview, NY: Cold Spring Harbor Laboratory Press, 1992), p. 29.

11. Kass, "Missouri Compromise" <http://www.agron.missouri.edu/mnl/79/05kass.htm> (August 9, 2005).

12. Ibid.

13. Kass, "Records and Recollections," p. 1256.

14. Lee B. Kass is the first McClintock scholar to discover the true facts behind McClintock's departure from the University of Missouri. See Lee B. Kass, "Missouri Compromise: Tenure or Freedom? New Evidence Clarifies Why Barbara McClintock Left Academe," *Maize Genetics Cooperation Newsletter* (2005), online 2005 <http://www.agron.missouri.edu/mnl/79/05kass.htm> (August 9, 2005).

15. Kass, "Missouri Compromise."

16. Barbara McClintock, letter to George Beadle, May 8, 1945, quoted in Margaret W. Rossiter, *Women Scientists in America Before Affirmative Action: 1940–1972* (Baltimore and London: The Johns Hopkins University Press, 1995), p. 242.

17. Letter from Nina Fedoroff to David Torsiello, February 27, 2005, in the author's files.

18. Sharon Bertsch McGrayne, "Barbara McClintock," in *Nobel Prize Women in Science: Their Lives, Struggles, and Momentous Discoveries*, 2nd ed. (Washington, DC: Joseph Henry Press, 1998), p. 163.

19. Bruce M. Alberts, "Please Come to My Laboratory for Better Coffee, Fresh Orange Juice, . . . Conversation," in Fedoroff and Botstein, p. 277.

20. James Watson, quoted in Victor McElheny, *Watson and DNA: Making a Scientific Revolution* (Cambridge, MA: Perseus Publishing, 2003), p. 23.

21. Barbara McClintock to George Beadle, quoted in Nathaniel C. Comfort, *The Tangled Field: Barbara McClintock's Search for the Patterns of Genetic Control*

(Cambridge, MA: Harvard University Press, 2001), p. 90.

22. Paul Berg and Maxine Singer, *George Beadle, An Uncommon Farmer: The Emergence of Genetics in the 20th Century* (Cold Spring Harbor, NY: Cold Spring Harbor Laboratory Press, 2003), p. 166.

23. Barbara McClintock, letter to Marcus Rhoades, December 7, 1949, quoted in Comfort, p. 143.

Chapter 7. "Jumping Genes" and "Controlling Elements"

1. Evelyn Fox Keller, *A Feeling for the Organism: The Life and Work of Barbara McClintock* (San Francisco: W. H. Freeman and Company, 1983), p. 114.

2. Barbara McClintock, "The Significance of Responses of the Genome to Challenge," Nobel lecture, 8 December, 1983, p. 181.

3. Evelyn M. Witkin, "Cold Spring Harbor 1944-1955: A Minimemoir," *The Dynamic Genome: Barbara McClintock's Ideas in the Century of Genetics*, eds. Nina Fedoroff and David Botstein (Plainview, NY: Cold Spring Harbor Laboratory Press, 1992), p. 116.

4. Evelyn M. Witkin, quoted in Keller, p. 126.

5. Nathaniel C. Comfort, *The Tangled Field: Barbara McClintock's Search for the Patterns of Genetic Control* (Cambridge, MA: Harvard University Press, 2001), pp. 133–134.

6. Barbara McClintock, letter to Charles Burnham, January 20, 1950 <http://profiles.nlm.nih.gov/LL/Views/Exhibit/narrative/harbor.html> (August 9, 2005).

7. Barbara McClintock, unpublished notes in

preparation for the Nobel acceptance speech <http://profiles.nlm.nih.gov/LL/Views/Exhibit/narrative/nobel.html> (August 9, 2005).

8. Nathaniel C. Comfort, *The Tangled Field: Barbara McClintock's Search for the Patterns of Genetic Control* (Cambridge, MA, and London, England: Harvard University Press, 2001), p. 167.

9. S. E. Luria, *A Slot Machine, A Broken Test Tube: An Autobiography* (New York: Harper Colophon Books, 1984), p. 34.

10. Barbara McClintock, "Introduction," *The Discovery and Characterization of Transposable Elements* (New York and London: Garland Publishing, Inc., 1987), p. x.

11. Keller, p. 140.

12. Comfort, p. 174.

13. The information about McClintock's letter of resignation to Bush, as well as about Beadle's and Bush's reaction, comes from Comfort, pp. 174–176.

14. Barbara McClintock, letter to J. R. S. Fincham, May 16, 1973 <http://profiles.nlm.nih.gov/LL/Views/B/B/G/_/llbbgc.pdf> (August 9, 2005).

15. "The Barbara McClintock Papers, On the Road: Lectures, 1954–1965" <http://profiles.nlm.nih.gov/LL/Views/Exhibit/narrative/lectures.html> (August 9, 2005).

16. "The Barbara McClintock Papers, Searching for the Origins of Maize in South America, 1957-1981" <http://profiles.nlm.nih.gov/LL/Views/Exhibit/narrative/origins.html> (August 9, 2005).

17. Keller, p. 143.

18. Barbara McClintock, "The Origin and Behavior of Mutable Loci in Maize," *Proceedings of the National Academy of Sciences*, vol. 36 (1950), pp. 344–355. Reprinted in *Classic Papers in Genetics*, ed. James A. Peters (Englewood Cliffs, NJ: Prentice-Hall, Inc., 1959), pp. 199-209.

19. Comfort, p. 208.

20. Keller, p. x.

21. E-mail communication from Maxine Singer, November 4, 2004.

22. Anna Marie Skalka, "A Tapestry of Transposition," in Fedoroff and Botstein, p. 173.

Chapter 8. One of the Intellectual Giants of Her Time

1. Gerald R. Fink, "Transposable Elements (Ty) in Yeast," *The Dynamic Genome: Barbara McClintock's Ideas in the Century of Genetics*, eds. Nina Fedoroff and David Botstein (Plainview, NY: Cold Spring Harbor Laboratory Press, 1992), p. 283.

2. J. R. S. Fincham, letter to Barbara McClintock, August 7, 1973 <http://profiles.nlm.nih.gov/LL/B/B/G/D/_/llbbgd.pdf> (August 9, 2005).

3. Joshua Lederberg, letter to science writer John Noble Wilford of *The New York Times*, October 11, 1983 <http://profiles.nlm.nih.gov/BB/A/Q/O/H/_/bbaqoh.pdf> (August 9, 2005).

4. Stanley N. Cohen and James A. Shapiro, "Transposable Genetic Elements," *Scientific American* (242), February 1980, p. 48.

5. James A. Shapiro, quoted in Sharon Bertsch McGrayne, "Barbara McClintock," *Nobel Prize Women in Science: Their Lives, Struggles, and Momentous Discoveries*, 2nd ed. (Washington, DC: Joseph Henry Press, 1998), p. 170.

6. Patricia Parratt Craig, "Jumping Genes, Barbara McClintock's Scientific Legacy: An Essay about Basic Research from the Carnegie Institution of Washington," *Perspectives in Science* 6, 1994, p. 31.

7. <http://profiles.nlm.nih.gov/LL/Views/Exhibit/narrative/nobel.html> (August 9, 2005).

8. Ernst Caspari, letter to Barbara McClintock, June 27, 1973, quoted in Nathaniel C. Comfort, *The Tangled Field: Barbara McClintock's Search for the Patterns of Genetic Control* (Cambridge, MA, and London, England: Harvard University Press, 2001), p. 241.

9. G. W. Beadle, letter to Barbara McClintock, November 20, 1981 <http://profiles.nlm.nih.gov/LL/B/B/D/V/_/llbbdv.pdf> (August 9, 2005).

10. Comfort, p. 245.

11. Kathleen Teltsch, "Award-Winning Scientist on L.I. Prizes Privacy," *The New York Times*, November 18, 1981, Late City Final Edition, Section B, p. 3, column 3, Metropolitan Desk.

12. John Noble Wilford, "Woman in the News: A Brilliant Loner in Love with Genetics," *The New York Times*, October 11, 1983, Late City Final Edition, Section C, p. 7, column 1, Science Desk.

13. Comfort, p. 252.

14. McGrayne, p. 173.

15. Nina V. Fedoroff, "Two Women Geneticists," *American Scholar* (66), 1996, p. 587.

16. Remarks of Evelyn Witkin, Barbara McClintock Professor at Rutgers University, at the memorial service held for McClintock at Cold Spring Harbor Laboratory, November 17, 1992 <http://www.nal.usda.gov/pgdic/Probe/v3nl_2/mcclinto.html> (August 9, 2005).

17. Barbara McClintock, letter to Frank Press, January 14, 1991 <http://profiles.nlm.nih.gov/LL/B/B/G/M/_/llbbgm.pdf> (August 9, 2005).

18. Nina V. Fedoroff, "Barbara McClintock: June 16, 1902-September 2, 1992," *Biographical Memoirs* (68), 1995, p. 230 <www.nap.edu/readingroom/books/biomems/bmcclintock.html> (August 9, 2005).

19. Fedoroff, "Barbara McClintock," p. 231.

20. Diane Ketcham, "A Tribute to Dr. Barbara McClintock, Geneticist," July 30, 1992, <http://thomas.loc.gov/cgi-bin/query/z?r102:E30JY2-39:> (November 22, 2005).

21. Nina Fedoroff, "The well-mangled McClintock myth," *TRENDS in Genetics*, vol. 19, no. 7, July 2002, p. 379.

22. Ibid., pp. 378-379.

23. Letter from Nina Fedoroff to David Torsiello, February 27, 2005, in the author's files.

Glossary

bacteriophage—A virus that attacks bacteria.

botany—The branch of biology that deals with the study of plants.

breakage–fusion–bridge cycle—Damage that some chromosomes experience repeatedly during each cell cycle.

chromosome—A threadlike structure found in cells of all organisms, made up largely of DNA and proteins, and consisting of many DNA units called genes.

controlling element—A mobile genetic element that functions as a switch to turn off and on the genes that express such physical characteristics as color or size.

crossing-over—The physical exchange of chromosome parts during cell division.

cytogenetics—The study of genetics through microscopic analysis of chromosomes.

cytology—The study of cells under a microscope.

DNA—The molecule found in all living cells that codes genetic information for the transmission of inherited traits.

epigenetics—The study of heritable changes in

chromosome structure or gene function that occur without changes in DNA sequence.

gene—Part of a cell that determines which characteristics living things inherit from their parents.

genetics—The branch of biology that deals with heredity.

genome—The library of genetic information that determines the development of living organisms.

Great Depression—Economic slump in North America, Europe, and other industrialized areas of the world that began in 1929 and lasted through the 1930s.

"jumping gene"—See **controlling element, mobile genetic element, transposon**.

maize—Indian corn.

microbiology—The study of microscopic organisms like bacteria, molds, viruses, and yeast.

mobile genetic element—A gene that can move from one place to another in the genome or from one species to another.

molecular biology—The study of large molecules involved in genetic information and cell function.

mutation—A permanent change in a gene or a chromosome resulting in a change in one or more inherited traits.

Nazi—Member of German political party that governed Germany from 1933 to the end of World War II.

Nobel Prize—Prestigious award founded in 1901 for outstanding achievement in physics, chemistry, physiology or medicine, literature, and world peace. A sixth prize, for economic sciences, was added in 1969.

nucleolar organizing region (NOR)—A region on a chromosome that contains the ribosomal RNA genes and associated proteins necessary for the synthesis of proteins in the cell.

radiation sickness—Sickness caused by exposure to nuclear radiation, associated with the breakage–fusion–bridge cycle.

RNA—A complex molecule that plays a major role in all living cells by helping produce proteins to build cells and carry out the cells' work.

synapsis—The pairing of chromosomes, one from each parent, during cell division.

telomerase—A protein controlling telomeres that affects both aging and cancer.

telomere—The protective cap at the tip of a chromosome.

transposition—The movement of a gene or set of genes from one DNA site to another or from one organism to another.

transposon—A mobile genetic element or "jumping gene."

zoology—The branch of biology that deals with the study of animals.

Further Reading

Books

Dash, Joan. *The Triumph of Discovery: Women Scientists Who Won the Nobel Prize*. Englewood Cliffs, New Jersey: Julian Messner, 1991.

Felder, Deborah G. *The 100 Most Influential Women of All Time: A Ranking Past and Present*. New York: Citadel Press, 1996.

Fine, Edith Hope. *Barbara McClintock: Nobel Prize Geneticist*. Berkeley Heights, N.J.: Enslow Publishers Inc., 1998.

Klare, Roger. *Gregor Mendel: Father of Genetics*. Berkeley Heights, N.J.: Enslow Publishers Inc., 1997.

Tracy, Kathleen. *Barbara McClintock: Pioneering Geneticist*. Bear, Del.: Mitchell Lane, 2002.

Internet Addresses

CSHL—History: Barbara McClintock
http://www.cshl.edu/History/mcclintock.html

Profiles in Science: The Barbara McClintock Papers
http://profiles.nlm.nih.gov/LL/

Barbara McClintock—Autobiography
http://nobelprize.org/medicine/laureates/1983/mcclintock-autobio.html

Index